About the Authors

Nick King is Head of Business Policy at the Centre for Policy Studies, a role he combines with running his own strategic consultancy, Henham Strategy. Nick is from Lancaster in the North West of England and came to London 'by accident' in 2006.

Nick was a Special Adviser in Government between 2012 and 2018, working for two Secretaries of State in three different Departments – the Department for Culture, Media and Sport, the Department for Business, Innovation and Skills and the Department for Communities and Local Government. In each of these Nick worked on policies to encourage local growth and economic rebalancing, including devolution, infrastructure investment, the launch of the Northern Powerhouse and the Midlands Engine (with which Nick still works), the creation of metropolitan mayors, distribution of the Local Growth Fund and the establishment of various Enterprise Zones.

Eamonn Ives is also a northerner who has made his way to London. He is a researcher at the Centre for Policy Studies where he specialises in business policy. Eamonn writes frequently for CapX, and has also featured in The Times, The Telegraph, The Independent, BrexitCentral, BusinessGreen and ConservativeHome among others. Before joining the Centre for Policy Studies, Eamonn was a researcher at the liberal conservative think tank Bright Blue.

About the Centre for Policy Studies

The Centre for Policy Studies was recently named by Conservative MPs polled by ComRes as the most influential think tank in Westminster. Its mission is to develop policies that widen enterprise, ownership and opportunity, with a particular focus on its core priorities of housing, tax, business and welfare.

As an independent non-profit think tank, the CPS seeks likeminded individuals and companies to support its work, but retains editorial control of all of its output to ensure that it is rigorous, accurate and unbiased.

Founded in 1974 by Sir Keith Joseph and Margaret Thatcher, the CPS has a world-class track record in turning ideas into practical policy. As well as developing the bulk of the Thatcher reform agenda, it has been responsible for proposing the raising of the personal allowance, the Enterprise Allowance, the ISA, transferable pensions, synthetic phonics, free ports and many other successful policy innovations.

Acknowledgements

We would like to thank the various ministers and MPs, special advisers, local authority leaders, business people and policy experts we talked to in the researching of this report. Particular thanks are due to Raytheon who supported the report. And thanks to the Institute for Policy Research who offered their support. We would like to thank James Heywood, Jethro Elsden and Archie Hill for their invaluable assistance in researching elements of this report. And we would like to thank Robert Colvile for his sublime editing skills which make every Centre for Policy Studies paper – including this one – so much more readable.

Contents

Executive summary

The United Kingdom's economy is unbalanced – with London and the South East dominating the picture.

It is in these parts of the country where a disproportionate amount of wealth is created and where the best paid jobs are typically found. Other parts of the country find themselves falling behind the capital and its surroundings, without the powers or funding to do anything about it.

The Government has recently focused on this agenda, with a new commitment to infrastructure and the promise, in the recent Queen's Speech, of a Devolution White Paper aimed at "unleashing regional potential in England and [enabling] decisions that affect local people to be made at a local level".[1]

This report, therefore, is intended to flesh out what a programme of activity to achieve the Government's ambition could and should look like. It evaluates the scale of the United Kingdom's regional imbalances, setting out credible and actionable recommendations which the Government should adopt in order to ensure that a rising economic tide can lift all regions of the country.

The report starts by examining ways in which the UK's economy is unbalanced, drawing upon data which shows the superiority of London and the South East in terms of investment, trade, growth and other metrics. We then lay out the principles which sit behind our proposals for "levelling up" – which put the emphasis on the devolution of power, so that local government can play a more active role in the local economy, and on a private sector which is incentivised to invest and operate in those areas which need it most.

Our proposals take as their starting point that the prosperity of London and the South East is vitally important and should be maintained as far as possible. That the UK can call upon economic powerhouses like these is a privilege. Little good would be achieved by impinging upon their ability to generate wealth and jobs and, as such, our proposals focus on levelling up, rather than flattening down.

With this in mind, we split the rest of the report into distinct sections, covering devolution, infrastructure, Opportunity Zones, and skills provision. Our recommendations are rooted in a positive belief that currently depressed parts of the nation could be performing better than they currently are, if only they had the chance to do so.

At times, these recommendations are deliberately non-prescriptive – because of the vital importance of allowing local actors the chance to forge their own path, experiment, and amend.

That said, we believe the following policies would go a long way to levelling up the British economy, allowing all to enjoy the prosperity our United Kingdom so readily generates:

---

1   Cabinet Office and Prime Minister's Office, 10 Downing Street, "Queen's Speech 2019". Link.

Devolution

1. **Embark on the next stage of devolution policy across the United Kingdom.** The UK's experience of devolution has been incremental and unequal. In some parts of the country, local governments enjoy extensive powers. Others do not enjoy the same suite of powers, while many more have scarcely been impacted by devolution at all. We therefore recommend that the long-promised Devolution Framework and the recently announced Devolution White Paper ensure a base level of devolution to all areas and offer clarity and more extensive powers to those areas or regions which would like to embark upon a process of more localised decision-making.

   Our analysis found that central government takes a far greater proportion of the total tax take in the UK compared to other OECD countries. It is therefore crucial that the next stage of devolution looks seriously at fiscal devolution. Local areas should be given some flexibility to vary different taxes, so as to allow them to become as competitive as possible.

2. **Developing localised transport and trade and investment policies.** Powers over transport are prime contenders for devolution and would likely be pivotal in helping to level up left-behind regions. More areas should be empowered to enjoy structures like Transport for London and new revenue arrangements to allow for the financing of transport infrastructure should be considered.

   London and the South East are head and shoulders above many other regions in terms of the amount they export to the rest of the world, and the amount of foreign direct investment they attract. We believe the Department for International Trade should rethink its remit, and work more closely with local promotional organisations, LEPs, business chambers, or pan-regional bodies to pioneer a localised trade and investment policy which gets businesses all around the country exporting more and tapping into the benefits which international trade can bestow, whilst also encouraging much more investment into the nations and regions.

3. **Leading from the front.** Demonstrating its commitment to regional growth and levelling up the UK economy, the Government should look to move some of its institutions and workforce outside of London and the South East. This would lead to a greater understanding of the issues facing different parts of the country, and therefore better policy-making.

Infrastructure

4. **Establish a new National Infrastructure Fund in the next Budget.** Infrastructure, particularly transport infrastructure, is critical for businesses to go about generating wealth and for as many people as possible to share in it. A new Fund should be set up, taking advantage of record low borrowing costs, to ensure the UK builds the infrastructure it needs for the future. The Fund should seek to leverage in private sector investment and expertise and, as well investing in transport infrastructure, also invest in energy infrastructure, electric vehicle infrastructure, space technology, digital connectivity and beyond. To ensure the Fund prioritises infrastructure outside of already well-catered for regions, namely London and the South East, we recommend that it is based in one of the UK's great northern cities.

Opportunity Zones

5. **Unleash a new wave of Opportunity Zones in disadvantaged parts of the country.** The new Government has already shown an encouraging appetite for creating free ports – a policy which the CPS is proud to have put on the national agenda. But areas which will not be nominated for potential free port status should also have the chance to benefit from more sympathetic business and tax regimes to allow enterprise to blossom within them. This should be done by creating a new wave of Opportunity Zones in deprived areas.

   If the Government wants to be more ambitious we suggest 'Opportunity Towns' are developed, where larger communities are able to exploit favourable rules which are conducive to enterprise and wealth creation.

Skills

6. **Improve educational attainment, and equip people with skills for life.** Academic attainment varies across the country, from early years through to further and higher education. Our research shows that schools in London and the South East deliver better average scores and that the capital dominates the list of schools most highly rated by Ofsted. To spread the success enjoyed in London and the South East, we recommend that the Government devolves more educational powers, for example by making the process of establishing Free Schools much easier, especially in deprived areas.

   Universities offer an obvious way to level up the economy and disperse high-calibre human capital to all corners of the country, given the healthy distribution of elite institutions around the UK. More should therefore be done to stem the brain drain which occurs upon students graduating, typically flocking to already economically successful places like London. For example, students should be encouraged to forge professional links with local employers while studying, and universities should facilitate this. Other policies local governments might wish to consider include attracting graduates into their areas through fiscal incentives.

Further education must not be overlooked in the push to level up skills around the country. Not only do FE colleges need to be held in greater esteem by policymakers, but they have to be delivering the skills which the workforce of today and tomorrow require.

We believe that the Apprenticeship Levy is not delivering the outcomes it should. There should be greater flexibility in how the pot of funds garnered by the Levy can be used – particularly with regards to supporting lifelong learning and the services sector. An overhaul of the Apprenticeship Levy, with flexibility permitted in those areas most in need of economic development, could help redress the balance and improve both skills and the service economy in the parts of the country which feel the need for them most keenly.

Taken together, these recommendations are credible and actionable and will go at least some of the way to levelling up the British economy. By harnessing the power of private enterprise coupled with local decision-making, we can unleash dormant prosperity in regions where it was lacking, while maintaining the coveted strength of the nation's existing economic powerhouses – ensuring that a rising tide truly does lift all boats.

Introduction

Our United Kingdom does not always feel as united as we might like.

Part of our nation's strength and appeal is down to the differences in background, dialect, culture and sport that exist around the country. But other variances might be considered weaknesses rather than strengths. One of the most obvious of these is the relative economic performance of different parts of the country.

While the UK can pride itself on being the fifth biggest economy in the world it is widely acknowledged that its economic strength is concentrated overwhelmingly in London and the South East.[2] Indeed, the UK boasts two of the three richest areas on the European continent – but also has sharper regional disparities than almost all of its major rivals.[3]

Of course, it is reasonable to expect differences in outcome to arise in a broadly liberal economy. The fact that people, companies, and regions do not experience absolute equality of outcome is a feature of our economic system, not a bug. It would be a nonsense to think that a prosperous society which experiences some inequality is preferable to one which is less prosperous, but perfectly equal. Besides, research suggests that greater levels of economic freedom are positively associated with economic equality.[4]

That certain areas will – and should be permitted to – do better than others is a long-established principle of economics. As Adam Smith remarked in his seminal work the Wealth of Nations: "There are some sorts of industry […] which can be carried out nowhere but in a great town", before explaining that in less densely populated areas, individuals must be a "butcher, baker and brewer for [their] own family" – his point being that the degree to which the division of labour, and hence the specialisation which so readily begets prosperity, is dependent on the nature of the geography and economy one is observing.[5]

The rise of modern technologies and new forms of connectivity, including transport and digital, mean the truth of this statement is no longer as self-evident as it once was. But the point stands that there are plenty of economic forces which may determine the success of a region developing or not.

But the story does not end there. Alongside market forces, there are political decisions which affect the relative economic performance and viability of an area. It is a fact of nature that the River Thames exists, that London was built on it, and its maritime history has led to much of its economic strength over the centuries. But it was chosen as our nation's capital, and the seat of Parliament, and much of its historic economic success comes as a result of those political decisions.

---

2   World Bank, "GDP (current US$)". Link.

3   Eurostat, "GDP at regional level". Link.

4   Nicholas Apergis, Oguzhan Dincer and James Payne, "Economic freedom and income inequality revisited: Evidence from a panel error correction model". Link.

5   Adam Smith, "An Inquiry into the Nature and Causes of the Wealth of Nations". Link.

Equally, the economic performance of an area can turn on decisions made concerning transport infrastructure or other types of foundational investment. Their economic destiny might also be shaped by the tier of government at which decisions affecting the local area are made and how close the decision-makers are to those affected by the decisions. Different local government structures abound around the country: again, these are political decisions leading to economic outcomes. And as Boris Johnson has repeatedly pointed out, many of our leading cities outside London are less productive and prosperous than the laws of economics would dictate.

In other words, where there are instances of economic imbalance which stem from, or are actively exacerbated by, government decision-making, there is a legitimate justification for action. Indeed, it is politically, socially and economically the right thing to do.

This is a stance which appears to have been adopted and prioritised by the new Prime Minister and the new Chancellor, both of whom have talked about their ambitions to "level up" the country and made devolution a central theme of the recent Queen's Speech.[6] Yet thus far, not much meat has been put on the bones of quite how that might be achieved. The aim of this report is to provide some stimulus to that effort.

---

6   Prime Minister's Office, 10 Downing Street, "Boris Johnson's first speech as Prime Minister: 24 July 2019". Link; Cabinet Office and the Prime Minister's Office, 10 Downing Street, "Queen's Speech 2019". Link.

The UK's economic imbalance – a snapshot

The UK's economic imbalance is not a new phenomenon. Plenty of academic studies point to London's long-standing dominance, even during times at which northern prosperity was at its greatest.[7]

Although the granularity and breadth of data enjoyed today only stretches back several decades, records allow one to identify broad economic patterns and trends. For example, we can see that gross domestic product (GDP) per capita in London has been head and shoulders above other regions within the UK from the late 19th century onwards – as illustrated in Chart 1, below.

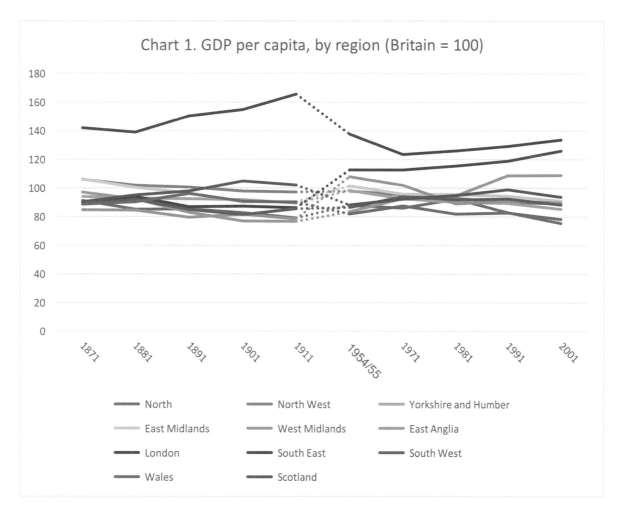

Source: Nicholas Crafts, "Regional GDP in Britain, 1871-1911: Some Estimates". Link.[8]

---

7   Ron Martin, "The Political Economy of Britain's North-South Divide". Link; John Bachtler, "Regional disparities in the United Kingdom". Link; Nicholas Crafts, "Regional GDP in Britain, 1871-1911: Some Estimates". Link.

8   Dotted line indicating gap in time series dates on x-axis.

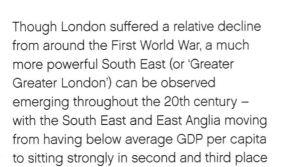

Though London suffered a relative decline from around the First World War, a much more powerful South East (or 'Greater Greater London') can be observed emerging throughout the 20th century – with the South East and East Anglia moving from having below average GDP per capita to sitting strongly in second and third place respectively.

This widening of the economic gap between the South East and the rest of the country is intrinsically linked to the decline of traditional manufacturing industries in Britain, and the transition towards a service-based economy. Signs of this evolution began to emerge at the end of the 19th century, but grew decidedly obvious after the end of the First World War.[9] As British manufacturing became increasingly exposed to the headwinds of international competition, profitability was duly eroded.[10] The newly developing world, replete with pools of cheap labour, was able to produce consumer goods like textiles less expensively than Britain's northern regions – which suffered accordingly.[11]

Meanwhile, industries which were once critical during the war efforts – for example, shipbuilding, and those associated with it such as coal and steel – saw demand dry up. Given that these were typically located in the Midlands, the North and beyond, the economic shock was felt most acutely there.[12]

As the 20th century progressed, Britain pivoted more towards light manufacturing and the services sector – including, importantly, financial services. Census data shows that the proportion of services jobs in England and Wales leapt from 48.8 per cent to 60.5 per cent between 1961 and 1981, while the proportion of manufacturing jobs collapsed from 36.3 per cent to 23.1 per cent.[13] Crucially from the perspective of regional imbalance, many of these new service jobs were located in, or close to, the capital. This is especially true of the best paid jobs, such as in the financial sector, which took off during Margaret Thatcher's premiership.

Gross value added (GVA) statistics bear out this geographic imbalance. These are a robust indicator of economic performance and can be calculated on a per capita and per region basis. As Chart 2 demonstrates, London stands out as the region with the highest GVA per capita by some distance – almost £20,000 more than the next region, the South East. Compared to the worst performing region of the UK, Wales, the average Londoner had a GVA some £28,000 higher in 2017.

Moreover, when we looked deeper into the figures, we found that the gulf between London and the rest of the UK has widened in the last two decades. In 1997, GVA per capita was on average 1.8 times higher in London than elsewhere in the UK. In 2017, however, that had increased to 2.1 times. In 2017, London had a GVA per capita at least double that of eight other regions of the UK, compared to just two regions 20 years prior. Incredibly, all regions bar the South East had lower GVA per capita statistics in 2017 than London did at the turn of the millennium, some by a considerable margin.

9   Ibid.

10 Michael Kitson and Jonathan Michie, "The Deindustrial Revolution: The Rise and Fall of UK Manufacturing, 1870-2010". Link.

11 Gregory Clark and Neil Cummins, "The Big Sort: Selective Migration and the Decline of Northern England, 1800-2017". Link

12 Ibid.

13 ONS, "Five facts about… The UK service sector". Link.

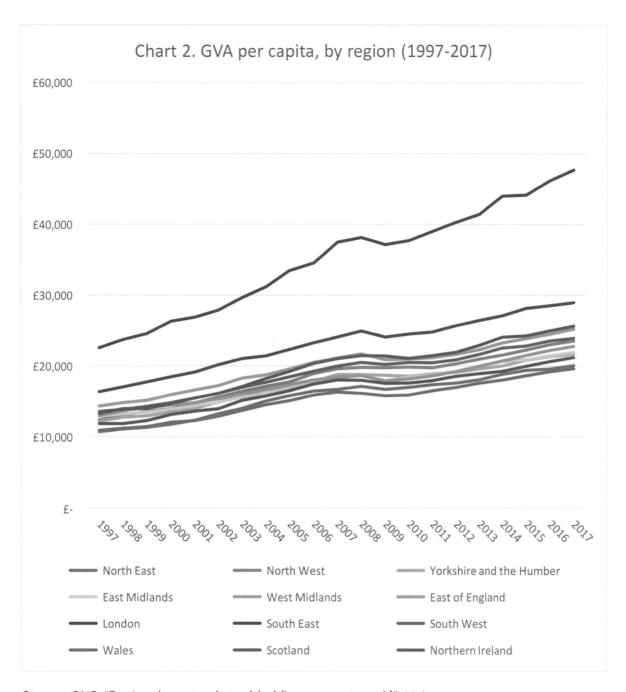

Chart 2. GVA per capita, by region (1997-2017)

Legend:
- North East
- North West
- Yorkshire and the Humber
- East Midlands
- West Midlands
- East of England
- London
- South East
- South West
- Wales
- Scotland
- Northern Ireland

Source: ONS, "Regional gross value added (income approach)". Link.

Unsurprisingly, these GVA figures are matched by data on earnings and gross disposable household income. Earnings in London range from being 1.24 times the second highest ranked region of the UK on this metric, the South East, to 1.45 times the lowest ranked region, the North East.

Even after taxes and benefits are accounted for, a sizeable divergence between gross disposable household income exists between London and the rest of the country, as illustrated below.

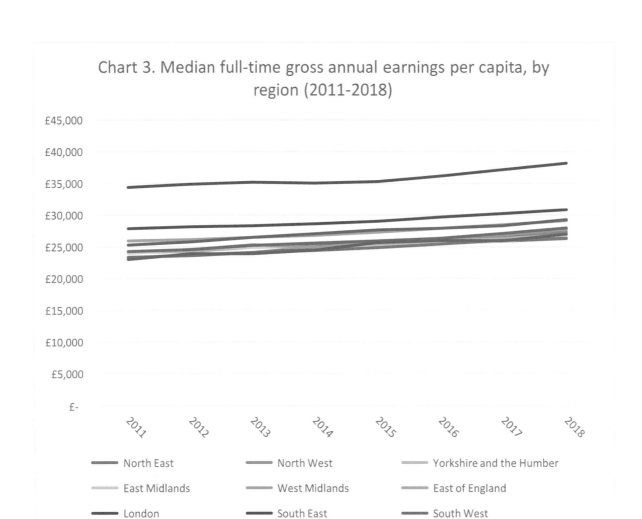

Chart 3. Median full-time gross annual earnings per capita, by region (2011-2018)

Legend:
- North East
- North West
- Yorkshire and the Humber
- East Midlands
- West Midlands
- East of England
- London
- South East
- South West
- Wales
- Scotland
- Northern Ireland

Source: ONS, "Annual Survey of Hours and Earnings time series of selected estimates". Link.

Chart 4. Gross disposable household income, by region (1997-2017)

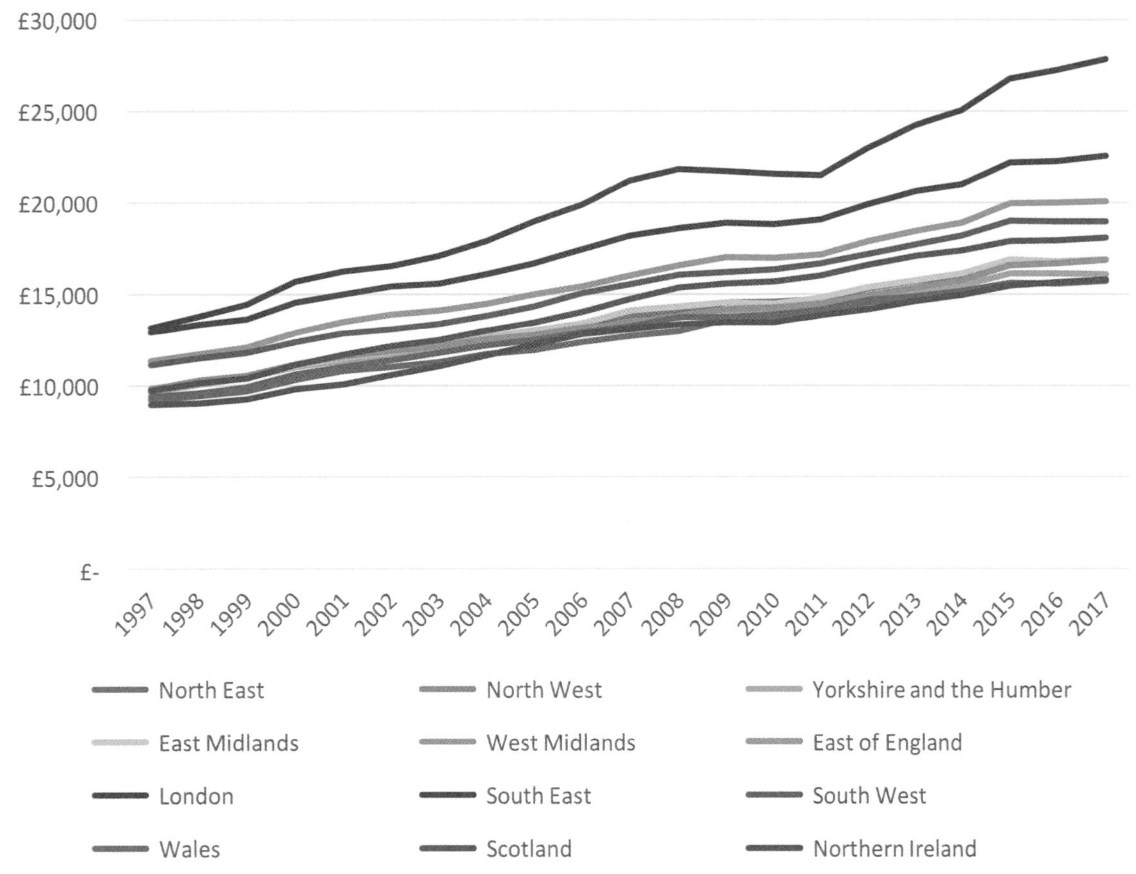

Source: ONS, "Regional gross disposable household income". Link.

We live in a country, in other words, where the capital dominates, and the South East succeeds alongside it. Many of the best paid jobs are situated in London and the South East, which duly encourages the most able to move there to meet the demand. In turn, that leads to greater productivity gains, and further government investment to ensure that potential is being realised. This further entrenches the relative economic success of London and the South East in particular.

The question, then, is what to do about it? How can we level up our economy so that other parts of the country can rival London and the South East in terms of economic performance?

Our approach

Regional imbalances in the UK economy cannot be traced back to one or even a handful of causes. Political decisions, geographic coincidences, international circumstances and plenty of other variables have collectively helped or hindered regions and their relative economic standing over time.

Proximity to European markets, for example, has been an economic blessing for London for centuries. Other geographic advantages have helped elsewhere across the country: natural endowments helped places such as Lancashire to grow wealthy, as abundant water and energy resources allowed the textiles industry to boom.[14] The establishment of elite academic institutions in Oxford, Cambridge or Edinburgh fostered research excellence which led to commercial opportunities and economic success in these cities and their surroundings. Some scholars even claim that the negative impacts of the Norman Conquest, which savaged much of the north of England nearly a millennium ago, can still be observed in the statistics today.[15]

All towns, cities, and regions should be allowed and encouraged to fulfil their potential. But poorer, and poorer-performing, areas should be helped to raise themselves up too. Ambition and aspiration should be causes for celebration – and ones which should be supported.

Research on spatial economic imbalance has a long history in academia, wider civil society and think tanks. Yet it has all too often (though not exclusively) been overseen by those with an overtly redistributive ideology in mind.[16] Specifically, policy proposals often tend towards arguing simply for increased spending.

Spending matters, of course – something we not only acknowledge but highlight by drawing attention to infrastructure spending later in this report. But it is not the be all and end all. Instead, there are three fundamental principles which need to be prioritised as we consider what will help poorer performing places level up.

The first is that there is a clear role for central government in helping particular areas fulfil their economic potential. Committed though the Centre for Policy Studies is to free markets and economic liberalism, we recognise that previous central government decisions have led us to where we are today and that future decisions – particularly legislative ones – can help level the playing field.

Yet although there is a clear role and remit for central government to create the conditions and framework within which local areas can flourish, our second fundamental principle is that decision-making is best done at a local level wherever possible. We think that local people, local places and local politicians should be given the means

---

14 H.B. Rodgers, "The Lancashire Cotton Industry in 1840". Link.

15 Gregory Clark and Neil Cummins, "Surnames and Social Mobility: England 1230-2012". Link; The Economist, "How Norman rule reshaped England". Link.

16 Tim Leunig and James Swaffield, "Cities Unlimited: Making urban regeneration work". Link.

                                       A Rising Tide: Levelling up left behind Britain

and incentives to support themselves. The UK is well-known for being one of the most centralised countries in the developed world and it is no coincidence that we are also one of the least well-balanced economically.[17] So where powers and responsibilities can be passed to a local level, they should be – for it is those closest to local issues and local people who are best placed to make the decisions which affect them.

Not only are there compelling epistemic arguments showing local actors can make better decisions than distant Whitehall mandarins,[18] but local decision-making – especially when applied in various policy areas, with different approaches being taken – spurs competition and fosters learning, which raises standards for all. By giving sub-national authorities the ability to experiment with rules, regulations, and taxes, the whole of society stands a better chance of finessing the practical application of governance in ways which more agreeably suit the general population.

The final principle is that it is business and enterprise which will make the most fundamental difference to a place's economic fortunes. What the success of places like London, Lancashire, Cambridge and Bristol has demonstrated over the centuries is that economic performance comes through the dynamism of, and opportunities created by, the private sector rather than the heavy hand of the state.

Within this report we have tried not to be prescriptive about the specific powers and responsibilities that ought to be held at specific levels in specific places, nor about what changes might most readily attract private sector activity within a particular area. It is our view that it is for local areas

to determine what steps might make the biggest difference locally. Indeed, given our support for trialling different approaches, and inherent competition between them, to stipulate the precise changes that must happen in local areas would be actively inappropriate.

International examples of devolved decision making.
There is compelling evidence that local autonomy can have a positive impact on economic growth. For example, German cities have much greater powers than their UK counterparts. Between 2000 and 2007, all eight of the largest German cities outside Berlin outperformed the national average in terms of GDP per capita and all 14 second-tier cities had better productivity growth rates better than Berlin. By comparison, in England, seven of the eight core cities have consistently performed below the national average in terms of GDP per capita.[19]

In Switzerland, competition between different areas on tax has been shown to highlight best practice and drive growth. Each of its 26 cantons has a separate, individually administered tax level. One study identified the example of Nidwalden and Obwalden, two neighbouring cantons of similar size: one pursued an attractive low-taxation policy and soon its GDP per capita was 44 per cent higher than the other, which had the highest tax burden in Switzerland. Obwalden soon realised that it was stifling economic growth and recognised the need to change policy.[20]

---

17 Institute for Government, "UK 'almost most centralised developed country', says Treasury chief". Link; Ben Gardiner, "The UK – an imbalanced economy". Link.

18 Friedrich Hayek, "The Use of Knowledge in Society". Link.

19 Core Cities UK, "A call for Greater Fiscal Autonomy for our Cities". Link.

20 Pierre Bessard, "Tax Competition: The Swiss Case". Link.

A recent OECD paper into decentralisation found a positive relationship between local autonomy and economic growth, concluding that "the analysis suggests that decentralisation tends to be supportive of economic growth".[21] It also noted in particular that "intergovernmental transfers", where local authorities receive most of their funding from the centre (which particularly characterise the UK), "are associated with slower growth, which could point at common-pool problems and a lack of incentives for own-source development".[22]

In other words, giving local areas power over their own economic destinies and allowing them to retain the benefits of growth is positively correlated with economic success.

Our recommendations, then, are rooted in an active but constrained role for central government, the devolving of responsibility and decision-making to the most appropriate level, and faith in the private sector as an unparalleled generator of wealth.

We believe that the analysis and recommendations which we will lay out in this report are credible and actionable – that they will work effectively, and be politically acceptable by both policymakers and the wider public. Combined, they can help ensure that all parts of the United Kingdom can enjoy the blessings of the economic prosperity witnessed in the best performing parts of the country's economy.

Because of the patchwork nature of devolution across the United Kingdom as a whole (discussed in more depth below) much of the content in this report will refer exclusively to England. But some ideas will apply across the United Kingdom as a whole.

This is, of course, a topic within which there is no shortage of possible levers to pull or proposals to put forward. But for the sake of the reader, we have limited our ideas to a relatively small number, each of which we think can help make a big difference in redressing the imbalances which currently exist.

Taken together, these provide a bold package of reforms which would make a huge difference to the UK economy. But they can also be taken in isolation: if some do not find favour with their intended audience, others might.

Each of these proposals is rooted in one or more of our guiding principles: that central government will typically need to provide the foundations for economic success, that decisions are best made at a local level wherever possible, and that the private sector is the only sustainable engine of growth for an economically disadvantaged area.

We start with devolution – because it is through local decisions, and a range of different decisions, that we can reap the benefits of competition, engendered by different approaches and generated through our understanding of the varying consequences.

---

21 Hansjörg Blöchliger and Oguzhan Akgun, "Fiscal decentralisation and economic growth". Link.
22 Ibid.

Devolution evolution – the next stage of devolution policy

The United Kingdom has undoubtedly become less centralised over the last 20 years. In 1997, referenda were held in Wales and Scotland, each of which saw majorities vote in favour of devolving significant powers from Whitehall to the respective nations.[23]

A year later in 1998, the Belfast Agreement was struck which similarly devolved powers to Northern Ireland, establishing the new Northern Ireland Executive and the Northern Ireland Assembly.[24] In England, successive governments have devolved powers to specific regions – such as Greater London, Greater Manchester and the West Midlands – and introduced metropolitan mayors in many of these areas.[25]

Yet by both historical and European standards, the UK remains extraordinarily centralised. As Ferdinand Mount points out in his book Prime Movers, at the start of the 20th century some 90 per cent of taxes in the UK were raised and spent locally, and only 10 per cent controlled by Whitehall. By its end, the proportions were almost exactly reversed.[26]

The Government has made it clear it is determined to change that – "to expand the benefits of devolution across England and put more trust in local people to choose what is best for their communities".[27] But how?

This section will focus first on the structures of devolution – in particular its distinctly patchwork nature – and then on some of the potential policy implications of devolved powers, particularly around finance and investment.

Currently, the spectrum of devolution in the UK is incredibly broad. At one end, one can find parts of the country in which there are parish councils with a small number of statutory powers. At the other, there is Scotland, with its own parliament, the ability to borrow hundreds of millions of pounds each year and responsibility for agriculture, health and social services and law and order.[28] The local government landscape, including that of the devolved nations as well as the Greater London Authority and the nine English combined authorities, is a hotchpotch of different bodies, with different powers and responsibilities.

But, as was famously remarked prior to the Welsh referendum on devolution by Ron Davies, the then Wales Secretary, devolution is a "process, not an event".[29] Many agree that there is much further to go – not least in terms of introducing some consistency and clarity on the options open to local areas.

The 2017 Conservative manifesto promised progress on this front, pledging "clarity across England on what devolution means for different administrations so all authorities operate in a common framework".[30]

---

23 National Assembly for Wales, "The History of Welsh Devolution". Link; The Scottish Parliament, "Past and Present". Link.

24 Northern Ireland Office, "The Belfast Agreement". Link.

25 House of Commons Library, "Devolution to local government in England". Link

26 Ferdinand Mount, "Prime Movers", Simon and Schuster, UK.

27 Cabinet Office and Prime Minister's Office, 10 Downing Street, "Queen's Speech 2019". Link.

28 The Scottish Parliament, "What are the powers of the Scottish Parliament?" Link; The Scottish Parliament, "Devolved powers". Link.

29 House of Commons Library, ""A process, not and event": Devolution in Wales, 1998-2018". Link.

30 Conservative and Unionist Party, "Forward, Together: Our Plan for a Stronger Britain and a Prosperous Future". Link.

A new Devolution White Paper was announced at the 2019 Conservative Party Conference, and again in the Queen's Speech, but the details so far are relatively high-level: we are promised "enhanced devolution across England, levelling up the powers between Mayoral Combined Authorities and increasing the number of mayors and doing more devolution deals". There will also be "more local democratic responsibility and accountability", with the White Paper containing details of "structural and institutional reform in England to support devolution and growth, in step with further funding".

Such commitments are welcome. Some disagree and point to the examples of Wales and Scotland (whose economic performance has lagged behind much of England) as an argument against devolution. The point that should be taken from these examples, however, is that bad governance and bad decision-making by political leaders will often lead to poor outcomes. This is precisely the sort of lesson which can be learnt as a result of devolution, showing which policies work and which do not.

Sometimes, governments and political decision-makers will make bad decisions, but we should draw a distinction between the ends and the means. It is adherence to the principles of devolution, coupled with implementation of the right policies at a local level, which will give local areas the best chance of future success and prosperity.

A Devolution Framework

At the heart of this devolution evolution should be the new Devolution Framework promised over two years ago. The deal-based approach to devolution which was taken during the Coalition Government and its successor governments achieved some

positive outcomes – which presumably is why the Government is promising to extend it. But it also led to a great deal of frustration on the part of central and local government representatives.

A new Devolution Framework should provide consistency and clarity for local areas, by drawing on certain key principles.

First, there should be at least a base level of devolution and representation which goes beyond that which currently exists. At the moment, organisations like the Northern Powerhouse and the Midlands Engine cover much of England – but there are swathes of the country which have no such representation. We support the recent calls to create a Great Western Powerhouse or a Western Gateway – but why not have similar high-level bodies cover the whole of England, and perhaps parts of the devolved administrations?[31] The roles and responsibilities of these organisations should also be formalised and made explicit, with powers and funding provided to ensure they are properly equipped to fulfil the mission set by central government.

The Government should however take care to ensure these do not follow the model and practices of the failed Regional Development Agencies, while recognising that some decisions, actions and interventions need to happen at the sort of scale which can only be provided by sub-national bodies.

Second, there should be clarity about what is on offer to local areas in return for reforms central government might want to see. To date, the new combined authorities have been rewarded with powers and new funding in return for collaboration between their local authorities and, typically, the election of a mayor. Local areas should be made aware of what steps they would need

31 Office of the Secretary of State for Wales, "Welsh Secretary – "Now is the time to create our own Western Powerhouse"". Link; Great Western Cities, "Britain's Western Powerhouse". Link.

to take in order to get new powers and/or funding devolved.

If the Government thinks certain powers can only safely be held at a county, unitary or combined authority level, it should say so – thereby giving local bodies the clarity they need.

Third, we support the Government's commitment to introducing elected mayors in England's leading cities. Although the first of the new breed of Metropolitan Mayors were only elected in 2017, the early signs have been promising – but most commentators would agree that they are limited in their powers and potential impact when compared to their international peers. The Government should therefore signal its support by looking to provide them with the same range of powers and responsibilities which are currently enjoyed by the London Mayor. But it should go further, looking to see what further powers might be devolved and which other areas might benefit from joint working through a Combined Authority and from the adoption of a directly elected Mayor in the future.

The Scottish Government should also look to introduce mayors in its leading cities, offering an all too necessary counterweight to the over-centralised administration in Edinburgh. The Scottish Government has appeared very keen on devolution of powers from Whitehall to Holyrood but has been less willing to devolve powers to its leading cities. It if is serious about devolution, it should rethink this aversion.

It has been noted that many local politicians and local people are uncomfortable with the idea of a directly elected mayor. They should be listened to and their concerns reflected within the framework that is published.[32] Which is why our fourth principle is that an alternative offer needs to be put forward outside the big cities which does not rely solely on the adoption of a mayor and which reflects and respects our historic county structures.

Finally, the role of Local Enterprise Partnerships (LEPs) should be re-examined. Undoubtedly there have been some successful LEPs, but even their most ardent supporters admit they have been inconsistent at best in terms of performance – and accountability remains a concern.[33] The publication of a new framework offers an opportunity to consider whether the powers and funding currently vested in LEPs could more appropriately be held at the combined authority, unitary or county level – or by other bodies entirely.

Yet the devolution framework is simply that: a framework. For local areas to really benefit from local decision-making, and the results of experimentation and competition, we need to go much further. In particular, local areas need to be given the keys to experiment, allowing them to unlock growth and economic opportunities and to stand on their own two feet.

Fiscal devolution and a new Devolution Bill

As we have argued elsewhere in this report, the UK is a highly centralised country – and there are few better examples than its fiscal system.[34] As Ferdinand Mount observed, a disproportionate amount of tax is collected at a central government level in the UK with England having "one of the narrowest and most restricted local taxation regimes" in the OECD.[35]

32 Centre for Cities, "Devolution and exiting the EU: Written evidence to the Public Administration and Constitutional Affairs Committee". Link.

33 Aileen Murphie, "Learning lessons from LEPs". Link.

34 Institute for Fiscal Studies, "Tax by design". Link.

35 Colin Copus and Steve Leach, "Let's talk about tax". Link.

36 Ron Martin, Andy Pike, Pete Tyler and Ben Gardiner, "Spatially rebalancing the UK economy: the need for a new policy model". Link.

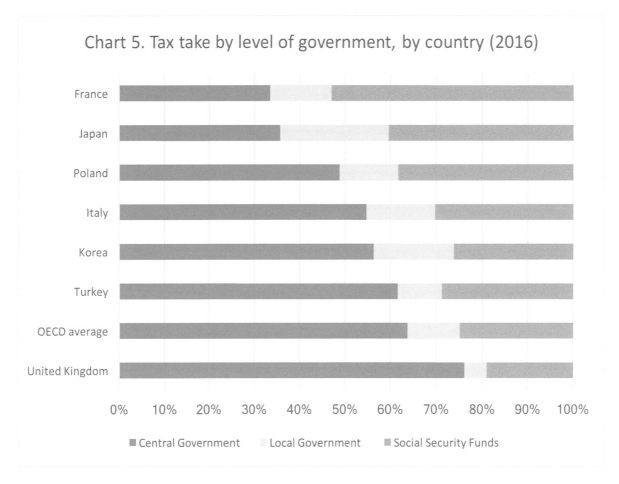

Chart 5. Tax take by level of government, by country (2016)

Source: OECD, "Revenue Statistics 2018: Tax revenue trends in the OECD". Link.[37]

The proportion of the tax take actually determined at the local level is equivalent to just 1.7 per cent of GDP, compared to 15.9 per cent in Sweden, 15.3 per cent in Canada and 10.9 per cent in Germany.[36] Notably, none of those countries suffers from the cavernous regional imbalances of the UK. take actually determined at the local level is equivalent to just 1.7 per cent of GDP, compared to 15.9 per cent in Sweden, 15.3 per cent in Canada and 10.9 per cent in Germany.[36] Notably, none of those countries suffers from the cavernous regional imbalances of the UK.

There are various taxes which should be examined for their suitability to be devolved to a local level. Perhaps most obviously, the

Government needs to make good on its promise to fully devolve business rates to local areas – and could return council tax to the hands of local leaders.

Beyond that, calls have been made for localised income and corporation taxes.[38] Edinburgh, Birmingham and others are asking to introduce new "tourist taxes" of the type which are commonplace around the world.[39]

Central government has been unstinting in its opposition to these – but this not only flies in the face of local autonomy, but suggests a lack of faith in the ability of centre-right politicians to make the case for low-tax, small-state jurisdictions. It also

37 Figures exclude supranational tax receipts for those countries which had them, and which in any case never exceeded 0.5 per cent of total tax take. The presented figures have been rebased accordingly.

38 Institute for Fiscal Studies, "Taking control: which taxes could be devolved to English local government?" Link; Fiona Morrill, "Devolving other national taxes to London". Link; Institute for Government, "Tax and devolution". Link.

39 BBC, "Edinburgh 'tourist tax' backed by council". Link; Matthew Daley, "Options for a tourism levy for London". Link.

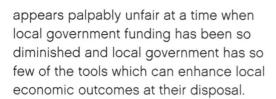

appears palpably unfair at a time when local government funding has been so diminished and local government has so few of the tools which can enhance local economic outcomes at their disposal.

To provide the means for this, we would support the passing of new legislation to devolve powers. An English Devolution Bill should be introduced which would provide the means for fiscal devolution with local areas and local actors having more say over both the range, and rates, of taxes in their local areas.

Some might fear that pitting local governments against each other in competition will lead to decreasing tax rates across the board and a lack of funding for the public services we all rely on. In reality, however, data suggests otherwise. An OECD report on tax competition between subnational governments, for instance, found "little evidence of a 'race to the bottom' with respect to tax rates and tax revenues".[40] But as in the Swiss example above, it has acted to deter those areas which have raised taxes excessively.

Moreover, even if tax rates were cut, this is not an argument to prevent citizens from having the freedom to choose what they demand from their local government and what they are willing to pay in return. In everyday life, we have premium and budget versions of supermarkets, clothing retailers, and transport options, with people given the choice of spending a little or a lot depending on the type of goods or service they want. Why should the council they choose to live under be different?

Improving the feedback mechanism between citizens and government would, in theory, lead to more responsive governments which are able to provide exactly what their citizens – as well as their

local businesses – want. Providing the means for local areas to set local taxes will make them much more responsive to the requirements of would-be employers and able to attract the private sector businesses which would enhance the local economy.

Devolved transport

As discussed elsewhere in this report, transport infrastructure is critically important to local development – and its funding is currently extremely unequal.

Leaving aside the issue of money (which we will discuss below), local authorities outside London currently have a relatively limited role in transport infrastructure. On the railways, for example, councils can contribute advice on pan-regional projects and can try to play a role in reopening or refurbishing local railway stations. In some areas they also have some limited capacity to subsidise services. In general, however, most big decisions on infrastructure investment are still made centrally by the Department for Transport, Network Rail, and other national bodies.[41]

The work done by Transport for the North and Midlands Connect show that much of the expertise and understanding of local transport challenges (and opportunities) now sits outside London. It is time for government to loosen the shackles of centralised decision-making and devolve power, responsibility and funding to such sub-national transport bodies.

Indeed, allowing other parts of the country to replicate organisational structures like Transport for London in their own regions should give them a stronger voice to access requisite funding and coordinate its delivery on the ground when they get it.

---

40 Hansjörg Blöchliger and José Maria Pinero Campos, "Tax Competition Between Sub-Central Governments". Link.
41 Government Office for Science, "Governance of UK Transport Infrastructures". Link.

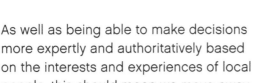

As well as being able to make decisions more expertly and authoritatively based on the interests and experiences of local people, this should mean we move away from the orthodoxy surrounding value for money assessments.

As has been remarked many times before, these rely on benefit-cost ratios which prioritise the journeys of those on high incomes or in areas where land values cost more – immediately favouring London and the wider South East – and frequently fail to capture the dynamic effects of major infrastructure projects.[42]

Putting decisions in the hands of local bodies would allow them to produce their own value for money assessments, more appropriately based on local circumstances. It would also allow local voices to be more readily heard and local support – or opposition – to be more easily taken account of.

As well as having funding and responsibility devolved to them, local bodies should have much more freedom to borrow in the same way Transport for London can, to invest and trial new methods of funding infrastructure projects – and, crucially, of attracting private investment and funding. Some progress has been made on this in recent years, with Manchester blazing a trail. The Manchester Metrolink is the UK's largest light rail network and has been voted one of the best in the world.[43] It is managed by Transport for Greater Manchester (TfGM), which was set up under the new Greater Manchester Combined Authority (GMCA) to bring together transport responsibilities from various areas under a single strategic body for the local area. The Metrolink has undergone significant expansion in recent years, including through TfGM's own resources and from borrowing.

As part of their funding settlements with TfGM, the GMCA have used their borrowing powers to finance projects including extensions to the Metrolink. A portion of the revenue stream from running the Metrolink is then allocated to covering the financing costs associated with the investment.[44]

Greater Manchester also benefits from an 'earn back' arrangement which gives it greater autonomy over transport investment. This model involves an ongoing revenue stream for Greater Manchester based on additional tax revenues generated from previous infrastructure investments. Not only does this give the GMCA and TfGM an incentive to maximise the economic benefits of investment, it also provides a "revolving infrastructure fund" for reinvesting revenues in new projects.[45] Such revenue has funded part of the expansion of the Metrolink.[46]

These opportunities are not available to all, but there is no reason why these sorts of models could not be extended to other parts of the country. Though plenty of transport infrastructure schemes are envisioned locally, they almost always require extensive lobbying of central government for funding before they can get off the ground.

If local areas can pool resources and risk by joint working, they should be able to borrow against future revenue streams: the 'earn back' approach can provide substantial funding for capital programmes locally.

42 Institute for Government, "How to value infrastructure: Improving cost benefit analysis". Link.

43 Helen Johnson, "Metrolink has been voted one of the world's best tram systems – but here's what you think about it". Link.

44 Transport for Greater Manchester, "Greater Manchester Transport Strategy 2040: Draft Delivery Plan (2020-2025)". Link.

45 Greater Manchester Combined Authority, "Greater Manchester City Deal". Link.

46 Transport for Greater Manchester, "Greater Manchester Transport Strategy 2040: Draft Delivery Plan (2020-2025)".

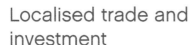

Localised trade and investment

The UK has long had an international reputation of being a good place to do business – a reputation which is endorsed by the World Bank rankings.[47] Relative to other parts of the world, British businesses enjoy reasonably low and flat taxes, efficient regulators, and – the obvious notwithstanding – stable political and financial institutions. That is one of the reasons that the UK has proven such an obvious location for foreign direct investment (FDI) over the years, consistently attracting more than other European countries.

As well as being a willing recipient of FDI, we are also a trading nation – and seeking to become an even more active one. While the vote to leave the European Union was about many different things, it is undeniable that the vision of seeing Britain trading more with the rest of the world – while retaining close links to European markets – has become a key theme in the wider debate. Indeed, given that as much as 90 per cent of global economic growth is expected to occur outside of Europe in the next 10 years, there is good reason to use Brexit to reset the UK's approach to trade to try to capture the rewards of that growth.[48]

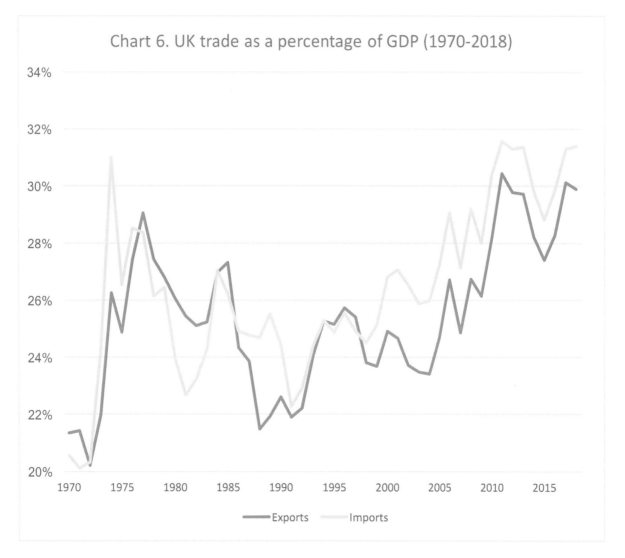

Chart 6. UK trade as a percentage of GDP (1970-2018)

Source: OECD, "Trade in goods and services". Link.

47 World Bank, "Doing Business 2019". Link.
48 Department for International Trade, "Britain's Trading Future". Link.

The UK is one of the most active trading economies in the world in terms of the value of goods and services it imports and exports. Over the past decades, both have steadily increased: in 2018, total trade stood at over £1.3 trillion, more than 62 per cent of GDP.[49]

But where trade and investment take place can have significant impacts for regional economic inequality. Exports are linked to beneficial economic outcomes – like higher productivity, employment, and wage growth.[50] Regions which export more goods and services are in a better position to capture those benefits. Similarly, those areas where there is more inward investment attract more and higher skilled

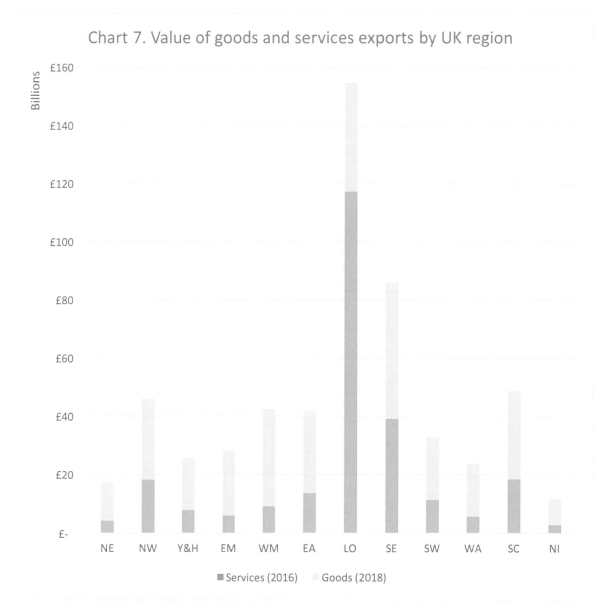

Chart 7. Value of goods and services exports by UK region

■ Services (2016)   Goods (2018)

Source: ONS, "Regionalised estimates of UK services exports". Link; HM Revenue and Customs, "UK Regional Trade in Goods Statistics". Link.

---

49 Department for International Trade, "Trade and Investment Core Statistics Book". Link; OECD, "Trade in goods and services". Link.

50 Matt Wheartly, "How do cities trade with the world? An analysis of the export profile of Britain's cities". Link; Francisco Alcalá and Antonio Ciccone, "Trade and Productivity". Link; Jeffrey A. Frankel and David Romer, "Does Trade Cause Growth?" Link.

jobs, as well as generating productivity gains which further entrench their dominant position. Once again, London captures the lion's share in terms of exports and FDI.[51]

A paper published earlier this year by the Centre for Policy Studies made a number of market-friendly recommendations about how to boost exports, with particular reference to how this could address regional economic imbalances.[52]

One of the issues that came out clearly when researching this report was that many of those we spoke to, including officials and Ministers within the Department for International Trade, thought that the reason that London and the South East dominate in terms of trade and investment is because of existing infrastructure, market access and 'brand recognition' – London is recognised around the world and is routinely considered in the same breath as New York, Singapore, and Hong Kong.

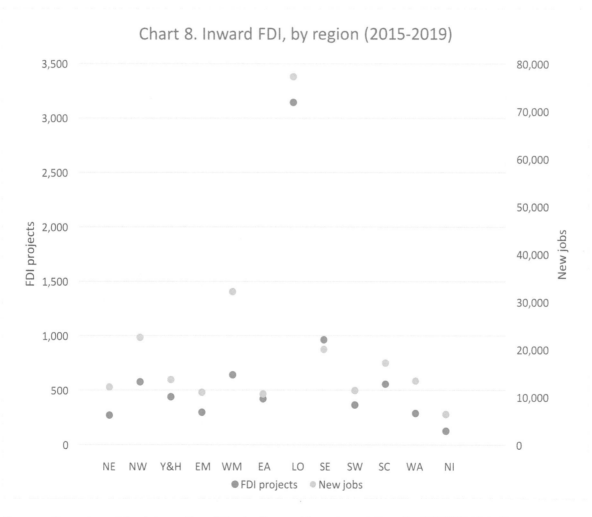

Chart 8. Inward FDI, by region (2015-2019)

Source: Department for International Trade, "Inward Investment Results 2015/16". Link; Department for International Trade, "Inward Investment Results 2016-17". Link; Department for International Trade, "Inward Investment Results 2017-18". Link; Department for International Trade, "Inward Investment Results 2018-19". Link.

---

51 ONS, "Regionalised estimates of UK services exports". Link; HM Revenue and Customs, "UK Regional Trade in Goods Statistics". Link.

The next section of this report shows how we can improve on the first of these. But progress also needs to be made in terms of both market access and recognition of opportunities outside London and the South East.

The issues here are at least threefold: there are not enough long-haul links from cities other than London to outside of Europe; there are too many businesses outside London who do not think they are capable of exporting; and there are not enough international investors who recognise the opportunities which exist outside of London and the South East.

The best way to overcome these challenges is for the Department for International Trade to loosen its grip on trade, export and inward investment promotion, and either devolve responsibilities and budgets entirely to the regions or work much more closely with them.

These funds could be controlled by local promotional organisations, the better performing LEPs, the Chambers or pan-regional bodies like the Northern Powerhouse and the Midlands Engine. But the most important element is to ensure local voices – including business voices – get a say in the allocation and proper spending of these funds.

Research conducted by Enrico Moretti at Berkeley shows that certain types of companies with a high reliance on technology and research capability – often those in advanced manufacturing and similarly skilled industries – are far more likely to drive productivity gains and economic growth.[53] Local actors need to be given the means to try to attract these sorts of companies to their localities. Business

voices are of particular importance as they will help ensure the funding is spent on the sorts of projects, programmes and wider activity which would most likely attract this sort of international investment as well as help develop and deepen trade links.

In time, this should help the regions of England, as well as the devolved nations, build profile, expand exporting opportunities and overcome the regional imbalance which currently exists.

A committed central government

The most important factor in determining whether or not the devolutionary principles and proposals outlined in this report will ever come to pass is, of course, central government.

As mentioned elsewhere in this report, the Conservative Government's commitment to devolution appeared to have stalled over the last three years – but with a new Prime Minister who was once the Mayor of London, and a Chancellor of the Exchequer who was once Communities Secretary and who used his Conservative Party Conference speech to announce a new Devolution White Paper, the topic of devolution is back on the political agenda.

That is welcome, but it only takes us so far. For the current attempts at devolution to be successful, all of government, including the Civil Service, must be four-square committed to the principles, implications and consequences of devolution.

That requires a serious culture shift on the part of a bureaucracy predicated on a Whitehall-first approach. Devolution, to date, has often felt like hard work on both

---

52 Eamonn Ives, "Tipping the Balance: How trade and investment can rebalance the UK economy". Link.

53 Enrico Moretti, "The New Geography of Jobs", Houghton Mifflin Harcourt, USA.

sides of the equation, with most transfers of power to local government seemingly resented by central government.

For it to work, then, will require resolve, determination and an enormous change in mindset.

The Civil Service should demonstrate their commitment to the devolution agenda. The various proposals outlined in this report offer some possible steps which might be taken in that regard, but there are other options which Whitehall might also consider.

Elsewhere in this report, for example, we talk about the UK having one of the most centralised systems of governance and decision-making anywhere in the world. That centralisation of decision-making is not just about the nature of the organisations which are making the decisions, but also about their geographical locations. As various academic experts, principally from the University of Cambridge, wrote in a report for the Regional Studies Association, "spatial economic imbalance in the UK has to do with the progressive concentration of [...] political [...] power in London and its environs".[54]

Supporting and enhancing its commitment to regional growth and levelling up the UK economy, the Government should look to move more of its institutions and workforce outside of London and the South East. Obvious candidates for this include parts of the Treasury, the Departments for Business, Transport and Trade as well as the Ministry of Housing, Communities and Local Government. The Government already recognises the need.[55] But progress has been slow to say the least.

This idea would show the Government is serious in its commitment to levelling up the British economy and would most likely lead to decision-making more sympathetic towards some of the inconsistencies present within the British economy. As the UK2070 Commission recently wrote of devolution: "If you will the ends, you must will the means: the rhetoric of devolution needs to be converted into action".[56]

---

54 Ron Martin, Andy Pike, Pete Tyler and Ben Gardiner, "Spatially rebalancing the UK economy: the need for a new policy model". Link.

55 Civil Service World, "Government to be set targets for moving senior civil servants out of London". Link.

56 UK2070 Commission, "Fairer and stronger: Rebalancing the UK economy". Link.

Building blocks – a new National Infrastructure Fund

People, communities and businesses need infrastructure to thrive. Much of the 19th century success of the West Midlands, for example, was built around its extensive canal network and the Victorians' buccaneering approach to railways, which opened up the whole of the UK economy.[57] In the present day, aviation links and digital connectivity are making the world smaller and new markets more accessible than ever before.

Transport infrastructure is often pointed to as a way of promoting regional growth and levelling up the economy – and for good reason. Improving the way in which people and goods can move around, and between, regions confers obvious benefits for commerce and wealth creation, such as increasing the speed and ease of doing business, while simultaneously lowering associated costs. Ultimately, research suggests that investment in transport infrastructure positively affects growth in labour productivity and total-factor productivity.[58]

Yet the UK's performance in this regard is not good enough. The World Economic Forum's 2018 Global Competitiveness Report, for example, ranks the UK 11th for its infrastructure. The WEF states that "inadequate supply of infrastructure" is the second most problematic factor for doing business in the UK.[59]

And when you look at transport infrastructure specifically, the UK's performance is even worse: we are in 15th place, putting us behind countries like France and Germany, but also below countries like Spain and Malaysia, which on a GDP per capita basis are significantly poorer than the UK.[60]

The Government acknowledges that expenditure on physical investment, which captures many forms of critical infrastructure, has been persistently low. According to a Treasury paper, investment in the UK as a share of GDP has ranked in the lowest 25 per cent of OECD countries for 48 of the last 55 years, and the lowest ten per cent for 16 of the last 21 years.[61]

Not only has the UK suffered from a woeful lack of investment in its infrastructure over many decades, but those infrastructure investments that have been made have tended to favour London and the South East. As mentioned above, more and more funding has gone to those areas which already have better transport provision. Specifically, London receives much more funding per head than other parts of the UK, with £944 being spent per person in 2016-17, compared to as little as £220 per person in the East Midlands – as shown in Chart 9, on the following page.

---

57 Gerard Turnbull, "Canals, Coal and Regional Growth during the Industrial Revolution". Link; B.R. Mitchell, "The Coming of the Railway and United Kingdom Economic Growth". Link.

58 Minoo Farhadi, "Transport infrastructure and long-run economic growth in OECD countries". Link; Nicholas Crafts, "Transport infrastructure investment: implications for growth and productivity". Link.

59 World Economic Forum, "The Global Competitiveness Report 2018". Link.

60 World Bank, "GDP (current US$)". Link.

61 HM Treasury, "Fixing the foundations: Creating a more prosperous nation". Link.

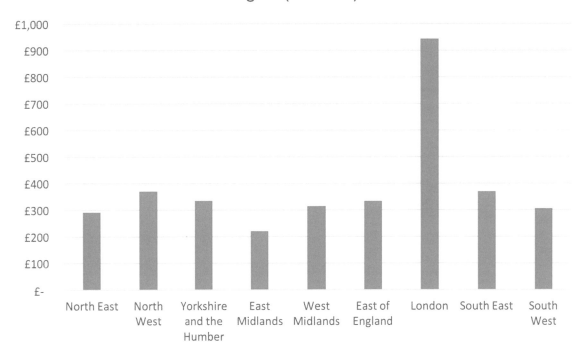

Chart 9. Public expenditure on transport per capita, by region (2016-17)

Public expenditure on transport per capita

Source: HM Treasury, "Country and regional analysis: November 2017". Link.

One can reasonably argue, of course, that there is more transport infrastructure in and around London and that is it naturally more expensive to maintain it – especially given the higher costs of land and labour in the South East. Furthermore, London can point to a sizeable difference in its resident population and its daytime working population.[62] Each day millions of people commute in from other regions and make use of London's transport. Similar arguments, too, can be made about the nearly 20 million tourists who descend on the capital from around the world each year.

But if anything these arguments underline the central concern: it is those areas which are already doing well which attract the lion's share of government funding. London has historically been invested in disproportionately compared to other parts of the country and this remains the case. In the last year for which figures are available, public spending per person was £10,323 in London, more than £2,000 more per person than the part of the UK with the lowest per person spend.[63]

---

62 Conrad Quilty-Harper, "Mapped: how the country's population changes during a work day". Link.
63 Philip Brien, "Public spending by country and region". Link.

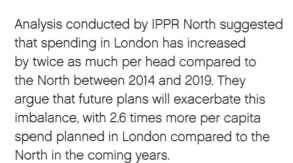

Analysis conducted by IPPR North suggested that spending in London has increased by twice as much per head compared to the North between 2014 and 2019. They argue that future plans will exacerbate this imbalance, with 2.6 times more per capita spend planned in London compared to the North in the coming years.

Decades of underinvestment in transport, and wider infrastructure, in vast swathes of the country have left them unable to keep up economically and have helped shape the regional imbalances we see in the UK today.

Yet the potential returns on infrastructure investment are well recognised. An IMF study found that an investment of an additional one per cent of GDP into infrastructure can increase output by 0.4 per cent in the year that investment is made and by a further 1.5 per cent in the four years following the investment.[64]

Figures from other organisations paint an even more compelling picture. The Civil Engineering Contractors Association (CECA) estimates that every £1 spent on building infrastructure raises economic activity by £2.84;[65] the CEBR found that every 1,000 direct jobs created by the delivery of new infrastructure boosts wider employment by over 3,000 jobs.[66]

Furthermore, the cost of borrowing is currently at record low levels – and ones which fall far below these expected rates of return. At the time of writing, UK 30-year gilts came in at well under one per cent (with even ultra-long, 50 year gilts yielding less than one per cent). In other words, the government can borrow at levels which fall beyond the expected

return rate on infrastructure investment and the expected rate of inflation. That means the real cost of borrowing money to invest in national infrastructure is below zero – and the Government should capitalise on that.

Sajid Javid, took the opportunity at the 2019 Conservative Party Conference to make good on his and the Prime Minister's admirable commitment to infrastructure investment by declaring the start of 'an infrastructure revolution' and announcing multi-billion investments into broadband and transport infrastructure.[67] But there is much further to go.

As part of the new National Infrastructure Strategy promised by the Government, a new National Infrastructure Fund should be created and delivered within the next Budget to invest in infrastructure projects up and down the country.

There is no shortage of potential projects which the new Fund could be used to support, as a cursory glance at the National Infrastructure and Construction Pipeline (NICP) and the National Infrastructure Commission's National Infrastructure Assessment will demonstrate.[68]

At first glance, this might sit oddly with the previous chapter's insistence on devolution. But the truth is that there will always be big, national infrastructure projects which central government will need to put its weight behind. Given the current fiscal settlement in the UK, it is also highly unlikely that local areas will have sufficient resources to tick off their infrastructure wishlists any time soon: they will still need to ask central government for

64 International Monetary Fund, "Is it time for an infrastructure push? The macroeconomic effects of public investment". Link.

65 Civil Engineers Contractors Association, "Securing our economy: The case for infrastructure". Link.

66 Ibid.

67 HM Treasury, the Department for Digital, Culture, Media and Sport and the Department for Business, Energy and Industrial Strategy, "Chancellor announces support for post-Brexit future". Link.

68 Infrastructure and Projects Authority, "Analysis of the National Infrastructure and Construction Pipeline". Link; National Infrastructure Commission, "National Infrastructure Assessment". Link.

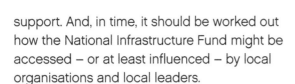

support. And, in time, it should be worked out how the National Infrastructure Fund might be accessed – or at least influenced – by local organisations and local leaders.

For example, you often hear people criticising the plans for HS2, which is suffering from the inevitable cost overruns. The Government's current review of the line is understandable: it is vital to get value for money. But those at the other end of the line, in the great cities of the North, are far more convinced by its necessity than those who dominate the debate in London – and even more so by HS3, dubbed the "Crossrail of the North". Funding HS2 and HS3 through the National Infrastructure Fund would provide vital connections to cities (and their hinterlands) whose economic potential goes unrealised, helping the UK develop exportable, best-in-class technology and skills while also delivering an economic benefit to our entire country.

But the new National Infrastructure Fund should not just invest in transport infrastructure but also into digital connectivity, energy and other utilities, as well as into the infrastructure to help us tackle climate change and to unlock and support new industries – in areas like space, cyber, and artificial intelligence – around the country.

The intention to do more in these areas was made manifest in the Queen's Speech where it was confirmed that there would be extra investment into science, with the Queen stating: "My Government is committed to establishing the United Kingdom as a world-leader in scientific capability".[69] Whether it is in terms of underpinning British expertise in space, virtual reality and augmented reality (which are expected to be worth £90 billion globally by 2024)[70] or biotechnology (a sector which attracted more than £2 billion

of investment in 2018)[71], the infrastructure is needed to ensure the UK can take a leading position in these industries in the future.

To ensure it is prioritising projects outside of London and the South East, given the ambition to level up the wider UK economy, the organisation responsible for administering the Fund would ideally be based outside of London and should be required to prioritise projects outside of London wherever possible. Smaller projects, for example connecting towns and communities to their local cities, are perhaps of even more importance in the context of levelling up the economy and reaching the most disadvantaged communities – and while it is local communities who will know best where the money should be spent, it remains for the time being central government that will have to provide the cash.

The Fund should therefore look to work alongside the National Infrastructure Commission as far as possible. And in so doing the Government should consider whether there is the potential for it to expand the remit for infrastructure from beyond the envelope it set the National Infrastructure Commission in its fiscal remit letter of November 2016 of 1-1.2 per cent of GDP envelope.[72] The OECD has suggested that global spend on infrastructure over the next decade should be about 3.5 per cent of world annual GDP.[73]

Of course, the UK has a more mature infrastructure sector than others – but also one that has been neglected. Notwithstanding the fact that much of that investment would and should come from private sector sources, there would still appear to be a need for the government

69 Cabinet Office and Prime Minister's Office, 10 Downing Street, "Queen's Speech 2019". Link.

70 Market Research Engine. Link.

71 UK BioIndustry Association, Confident capital: backing UK biotech. Link.

72 Philip Hammond, "Remit letter for National Infrastructure Commission (NIC)". Link.

73 OECD, "Fostering Investment in Infrastructure: Lessons learned from OECD Investment Policy Reviews". Link.

to invest more, especially given the historic lack of investment outlined above. This requirement is all the more pressing given that when the UK leaves the European Union it will no longer be a member of the European Investment Bank (EIB),[74] which has provided more than €44.2 billion of funding for UK infrastructure projects between 2010 and when this report was published.[75]

There will be those who dislike the idea of the government borrowing tens, if not hundreds, of billions of pounds on a point of principle. But at a time when borrowing costs are so low, growth is anaemic, and the regional imbalance within the UK is so serious, there is a compelling case for it. That case is recognised by the British public: some 75 per cent of British adults think that more needs to be spent on improving the UK's core infrastructure networks.[76]

These infrastructure investments will be made in productive parts of the economy which will deliver concrete long-term benefits (and which would be all the more important if the UK is tipped into a recession as part of a wider global economic collapse). The National Infrastructure Fund will allow the Government and others to take the long-term investment decisions which will help the UK secure its post-Brexit future.

It is vital, however, that the Government does not just pour public money into this – however cheap the cost of borrowing – but looks to use innovative financing models like 'land value capture', and seeks to bring in as much private-sector funding alongside as possible. There are various models for this which could be pursued including concession models (as used for High Speed 1) and the Regulated Asset Base model (recently used to finance the Thames Tideway Tunnel). Wherever possible, these infrastructure investments should – and will – pay for themselves both directly and indirectly.

Offering investors the opportunity to take direct stakes in the infrastructure which will underpin the UK's changing economy can help increase the size of the investment pot, but will also bring in expert resource from the private sector to curb unwise government spending and will offer institutional investors a stake in the long-term success of the UK economy.

Infrastructure has been neglected for far too long in this country, with successive governments seemingly lacking the appetite and the means to get projects off the ground. With the current administration it feels like the appetite might finally be there. A National Infrastructure Fund would provide the means of funding it.

74 HM Treasury and the Infrastructure and Projects Authority, "Infrastructure Finance Review: consultation". Link.
75 European Investment Bank, "Financed projects". Link.
76 Institution of Civil Engineers, "State of the Nation 2018: Infrastructure Investment". Link.

Opportunity knocks – a new category of Opportunity Zones

Given the centralised nature of the UK in general and England in particular, one can safely assume there are likely to be some limits on how far central government would go in the near future in terms of adopting a new, universally applied system of devolution that lets local areas have broad, sweeping powers to trial different approaches and control their own taxation base.

There remains a clear case, therefore, for central government to provide a means for those areas with a particular need to become more economically active.

The idea that special, targeted measures might be undertaken in specific parts of the UK where help is most needed – perhaps where generations have been locked out of work, where employment opportunities are scarce, and where hope appears to be lost – is not a new one. But it is one which needs refreshing.

Margaret Thatcher encouraged, and successive governments since 2010 have continued to push, Enterprise Zones as the most appropriate way to help encourage private sector activity in a specific area.[77] Thatcher's Enterprise Zones offered exemptions from industrial and commercial property rights and taxes on land, and 100 per cent allowances on capital expenditure on buildings.[78] They also had simplified planning regimes, and reduced the amount

of government-imposed bureaucracy imposed through statistical information requests and the like.[79]

Perhaps the most successful Enterprise Zone was the Isle of Dogs in London, which today famously plays host to much of the country's financial sector.

Eventually, these Zones had to be phased out, largely due to regulations stemming from the European Commission.[80] But that did not stop the former Chancellor, George Osborne, reviving a new form of Enterprise Zones when the Coalition Government came to power.[81] By 2015, 24 Enterprise Zones were established across England, and a further 18 were announced that year.[82]

Businesses which moved into Enterprise Zones before the end of the 2010-2015 parliament could benefit from a 100 per cent business rate discount worth up to £275,000 over a five-year period, simplified planning regulations and access to government support to ensure they could receive superfast broadband.[83]

These Enterprise Zones should be seen as a step in the right direction. But ultimately, they were lacking in vision and impact. The need to go further was one of the catalysts behind the Centre for Policy Studies' proposal to establish free ports in some of the UK's most deprived areas once

---

77 Matthew Ward, "Enterprise Zones". Link.

78 Ibid.

79 Ibid.

80 HC Deb (4 Jun 1996, c385). Link.

81 HM Treasury and the Department for Business, Innovation and Skills, "The Plan for Growth". Link.

82 Ministry of Housing, Communities and Local Government, "The New Enterprise Zones". Link.

83 Ibid.

Britain was outside of the EU – an idea first proposed in 2016 by Rishi Sunak MP, now Chief Secretary to the Treasury, in The Free Ports Opportunity.[84] This message has been heard by Boris Johnson, who pledged to bring forward a series of free ports upon becoming Prime Minister.[85]

If Britain's free ports were as successful as those in the USA, the UK could expect to see over 86,000 jobs created. And these jobs would be in the places which need them most. Sunak's paper explained that 17 of the UK's 30 largest ports were in the bottom quartile of local authorities as ranked by the Index of Multiple Deprivation.[86]

But these free ports would, typically, be located around ports themselves. Suitable candidates for help and support, certainly, but by no means the only ones. A new generation of Opportunity Zones would offer the chance to do something just as ambitious, if not even more so, up and down the land.

A useful model for this exists in the United States, where, through the American Tax Cuts and Jobs Act 2017, more than 8,700 such areas were created.[87] The American model offers preferential tax conditions for individuals and corporations in such areas.[88] In simple terms, investors can reinvest capital gains into a Qualified Opportunity Fund (QOF), and both defer and reduce their tax liability. After five years, the deferred tax is reduced by ten per cent; after seven, by a further five per cent.

If the investor still holds their investment after a decade then they are eligible for the increase in their QOF investment based on fair market value.[89]

While the investment is being sheltered in the QOF, the Fund can finance a range of different activities or projects within its geographical jurisdiction – such as on housing, infrastructure, and start-up businesses.

In sum, therefore, Opportunity Zones appear to be a win-win policy – investors can reduce their tax liability, and distressed areas get an injection of capital with which to kickstart their local economies.

The UK Government should however learn from the American example, because US Opportunity Zones have not been without their critics. Some are opposed to them because they think the means by which they are chosen is inappropriate or misguided,[90] whereas others think that they simply subsidise investment which would have occurred otherwise,[91] or that they can lead to perverse outcomes which will not necessarily help local areas.[92]

But it should be recognised that many of the criticisms of Opportunity Zones lie more in their application than their inherent nature. The Government should therefore examine the American model closely to see what amendments it might want to make regarding how they work and what might be permitted to occur within each Opportunity Zone.

84 Rishi Sunak, "The Free Ports Opportunity: How Brexit could boost trade, manufacturing and the North". Link.

85 Jess Shankleman, "Boris Johnson Widens Push for Singapore-Style Free Ports in U.K." Link; HM Treasury and the Department for International Trade, "Trade Secretary announces Freeports Advisory Panel will ensure UK is ready to trade post-Brexit". Link.

86 Rishi Sunak, "The Free Ports Opportunity: How Brexit could boost trade, manufacturing and the North". Link.

87 Tax Cuts and Jobs Act 2017. Link; Tax Policy Center, "Briefing Book: A citizen's guide to the fascinating (though often complex) elements of the federal Tax System". Link.

88 Ibid.

89 Inland Revenue Service, "Opportunity Zones Frequently Asked Questions". Link.

90 Scott Eastman, "Measuring Opportunity Zone Success". Link.

91 Scott Eastman and Nicole Kaeding, "Opportunity Zones: What We Know and What We Don't". Link.

92 Tax Policy Center, "Briefing Book: A citizen's guide to the fascinating (though often complex) elements of the federal Tax System". Link; Scott Eastman, "Measuring Opportunity Zone Success". Link.

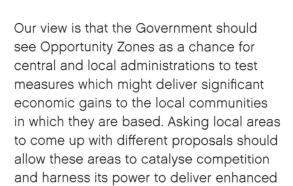

Our view is that the Government should see Opportunity Zones as a chance for central and local administrations to test measures which might deliver significant economic gains to the local communities in which they are based. Asking local areas to come up with different proposals should allow these areas to catalyse competition and harness its power to deliver enhanced outcomes.

Examples might include measures which the Centre for Policy Studies has previously called for, such as a Simple Consolidated Tax (SCT) – a voluntary tax system which businesses with annual revenues of under £1,000,000 could opt into instead of paying Corporation Tax, Employer's National Insurance, VAT and business rates[93] – or the introduction of 'full expensing'.

This, in the USA, was another component of the Tax Cuts and Jobs Act 2017. Full expensing allows businesses to deduct the full cost of qualified new investments in the year they were made.[94] This ensures that businesses are able to offset the full cost of their investment against tax – without the gains being eroded away by inflation and opportunity costs.[95] It therefore boosts investment, and, importantly, is a tax benefit reaped only by companies investing in productive capital like machinery.

The estimated economic effects of full expensing are staggering, with one economist calculating that it increased investment by 17.5 per cent and wages by 2.5 per cent in those states which made use of it in America.[96]

From the perspective of economic rebalancing, one of the main benefits of full expensing is that the advantages of it naturally accrue to capital-intensive firms, such as those in the manufacturing sector. As poorer regions of the UK tend to host more manufacturing firms, they would likely be the big winners were the policy to be introduced in Opportunity Zones.

In addition to experimenting with full expensing or the Simple Consolidated Tax, local areas might look to – and be permitted to – reduce or abolish business rates or employers' National Insurance, relax planning rules or offer financial incentives or support for skills or renovation of old or unwanted housing.

To ensure the most effective and compelling ideas are brought forward, local areas should be encouraged – or perhaps even mandated – to work with the private sector to inform their proposals. This would be the most successful way of unlocking new investment but also of ensuring that existing businesses can grow within a supportive commercial environment.

As a general principle, the Government should target these Opportunity Zones specifically at those areas which are the least economically well-off, allowing those companies moving into them to benefit from lower taxes and less regulation. A possible means would be to use the Index of Multiple Deprivation (IMD), which breaks up local authorities into 'lower super output areas' (LSOA). It could be stipulated that only LSOAs in the bottom ten per cent of the IMD ranking could qualify, for example.

Alternatively, if a more ambitious approach was favoured, an Opportunity Zone could consist of a much wider geographical area.

93 Nick King, "Think Small: A blueprint for supporting UK small businesses". Link.
94 Tax Policy Center, "How did the Tax Cuts and Jobs Act change business taxes?" Link.
95 Sam Bowman, "Full expensing: The best idea in politics you've never heard of". Link.
96 Eric Ohrn, "The Effect of Tax Incentives on U.S. Manufacturing: Evidence from State Accelerated Depreciation Policies". Link.

There is no reason why entire towns, or coastal communities, might not benefit from a more business-friendly approach. The advancement of 'Opportunity Towns' would serve as a natural corollary of, or extension to, the Government's recently announced Stronger Towns Fund.

Indeed, there is an argument for looking at even larger areas for the Opportunity Zones. As mentioned above, the most successful example of an Enterprise Zone was the Isle of Dogs. That and the regeneration of the Liverpool Docklands show the benefits of working at scale, with innovative approaches.

There should be no prescriptive approach towards what these new Opportunity Zones might look to do. The Government should instead look to ask local areas what they want and what powers, responsibilities and abrogations would make a difference locally. We hope the forthcoming Devolution White Paper will provide the means with which to ask that question.

Shoot to skill – enhancing the skills base

People are the lifeblood of any economy. Economies exist because of, and for, the people they comprise. As such, human capital should be regarded as the most important factor of production – without it, there would be nothing to bring together the capital and resources which ultimately generate wealth in society.

Suffice to say, the quality of human capital – for example, the relative skills and talents of a labour force – has a powerful determining influence on the success of an economy.[97]

A clear indicator of human capital is educational attainment. As may be expected, the UK can boast a comparatively well-educated population. Even among OECD countries, the UK consistently scores above average in standardised, worldwide attainment ranking surveys.[98]

Yet, just as is the case with the wider economic picture, significant differences exist between regions of the UK at various points within the education cycle, with London and South East typically coming out on top.

Levelling up schools

Regional imbalances in educational attainment start in the earliest years of schooling – if not before.[99] Between the home nations, for example, the evidence suggests that English pupils typically demonstrate the highest aptitude in reading, mathematics, and science, followed by those from Northern Ireland, Scotland and then Wales.[100] This is not down to any innate superiority, but the structure of their respective education systems.

Statistics for educational attainment are also available on a local authority level which allows for more granular analysis. Due to differing educational systems, UK-wide comparisons cannot be made. However, in England, one can see how educational attainment at GCSE and equivalent level is typically higher among pupils from London and the South East.

While students in the North East typically gained an Attainment 8 score of 44.7, their counterparts in London and the South East achieved scores of 49.2 and 47.7 respectively. Moreover, our analysis of data for Attainment 8 scores of state educated children shows that 80 per cent of the top ten performing local authorities are located in London and the South East. Only one local authority across all northern regions – Trafford – manages to break into this elite bracket.

97 Muhammad Ali, Abiodun Egbetokun and Mazoor Hussain Memom, "Human Capital, Social Capabilities and Economic Growth". Link.
98 OECD, "Programme for International Student Assessment (PISA) results from PISA 2015: United Kingdom". Link.
99 National Foundation for Educational Research, "Key insights from PISA 2015 for the UK nations". Link.
100 Ibid.

Chart 10. Average Attainment 8 score, by region (2017-18)

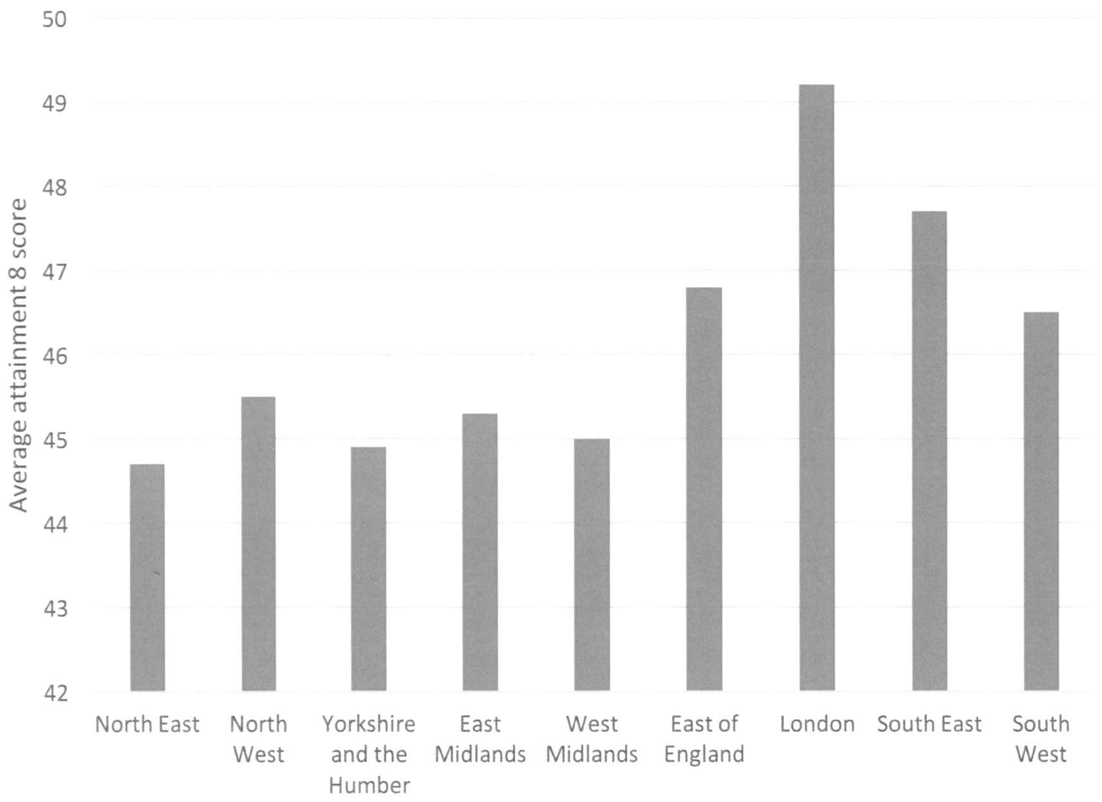

Bar chart showing average attainment 8 score by region. Y-axis "Average attainment 8 score" ranges from 42 to 50. Approximate values: North East 44.7, North West 45.5, Yorkshire and the Humber 44.9, East Midlands 45.3, West Midlands 45.0, East of England 46.8, London 49.2, South East 47.7, South West 46.5.

Source: Department for Education, "GCSE and equivalent results in England 2017/18 (provisional)".
Link.

Ofsted data also allows one to compare the quality of schools by local authority or region. If you take schools being judged as "Outstanding" or "Good" as obvious indicators of good performance, the wide disparity in quality between regions is further demonstrated. In London, 92 per cent of schools are rated as such, as are 89 per cent of the South East's, compared to just 80 per cent of those in Yorkshire and the Humber, and 81 per cent of those in the South West.

Yet London's experience makes for an interesting case study – because in contrast to other areas, this is not somewhere where the capital has enjoyed a long-running, self-entrenching advantage.

Not long ago, pupils in London – especially inner London – lagged behind their counterparts in the rest of England.[101] In the early 2000s, the proportion of inner London pupils achieving five or more GCSEs at A* to C grade (including English and Maths) was around 35 per cent whereas for the rest of England, it was closer to 50 per cent.[102] But within 10 years that gap had all but disappeared. Among the most disadvantaged children – those receiving free school meals – the progress made was remarkably better than those across the rest of the country.[103]

---

101 Jo Blanden, Ellen Greaves, Paul Gregg, Lindsay Macmillan and Luke Sibieta, "Understanding the improved performance of disadvantaged pupils in London". Link.

102 Ibid.

103 Ibid.

Such a radical improvement has naturally led to examination of how it occurred.[104] Unsurprisingly, research suggests that this turnaround in educational attainment cannot be attributed to a single factor.[105] But many believe that attainment was increased and success was achieved by breaking down the centralised nature of educational provision and by allowing for experimentation.[106] A report by the Centre for Analysis of Social Exclusion and the London School of Economics states that the abolition of the Inner London Educational Authority (a pan-borough organisation) may have accelerated London's progress as educational responsibilities were transferred to individual boroughs.[107] But there was also a wider move towards academisation during this time.[108] Academies are government-funded schools but are exempt from local authority control. Such schools have been found to improve education outcomes, and their existence as a competitor to state-managed schools drives up standards across the board.[109]

These arguments fit within our firm belief that localism and experimentation foster success. Applying the lessons learnt from London to the rest of the country should, in turn, help these areas raise their standards and achieve more success. In a recent CPS report, Suella Braverman MP highlighted the relative success of free schools – which build on the policy of academy schools – and called for the process of establishing them to be accelerated.[110] Pleasingly, soon after her report was published, Boris Johnson stated his intention to create 30 new Free Schools.[111]

Reforms like this are, we believe, crucial to ensuring that the educational system across the UK is as good as it can be. Not only will the new schools likely be attractive places for parents, but they should also drive up standards elsewhere – benefiting everybody.

Of course, more wholesale, nationally focused, reforms will be critical too. This is especially true in terms of redressing long-term structural problems which have led to the quality of Britain's educational system falling short of its true potential. Encouragingly, the new administration appears to be making welcome progress here.

In September, the new Education Secretary, Gavin Williamson, announced that starting salaries for new teachers would rise to £30,000 by 2022-23.[112] This boost will be critical to ensuring that the best candidates to become teachers are attracted into the profession. Yet from the perspective of seeking to equalise regional education attainment, it might have been even better to award such salary rises on a sliding scale, with more going to those teachers who are working in the most challenging schools and the regions which need levelling up. Nevertheless, given the increased appeal of a starting salary of £30,000 outside the capital, one might reasonably hope and expect it to help drive up standards in those parts of the country which need that most.

104 Chris Cook, "London schools rise to the challenge". Link; BBC, "'Startling turnaround' transforms London state schools". Link; The King's Fund, "The London Challenge". Link.

105 Alex Hill, Liz Mellon, Jules Goddard and Ben Laker, "How to Turn Around a Failing School". Link.

106 Marc Kidson and Emma Norris, "Implementing the London Challenge". Link; Merryn Hutchings, "Why is attainment higher in London than elsewhere?" Link.

107 Jo Blanden, Ellen Greaves, Paul Gregg, Lindsay Macmillan and Luke Sibieta, "Understanding the improved performance of disadvantaged pupils in London". Link.

108 Tony McAleavy and Alex Elwick, "School improvement in London: a global perspective". Link.

109 National Audit Office, "Managing the expansion of the Academies Programme". Link; National Audit Office, "The Academies Programme". Link.

110 Suella Braverman, "Fight for Free Schools". Link.

111 John Johnston, "Boris Johnson vows to create thousands more school places in bid to 'drive up standards'". Link.

112 Department for Education, "£30,000 starting salaries proposed for teachers". Link.

Spreading graduate provision

The imbalances observable in primary and secondary education are, of course, mirrored within higher education (HE).

The top five universities in the UK are Cambridge, Oxford and three London universities – all based in relatively affluent parts of the country.[113] There are, of course, prestigious universities situated across the country – in fact, every region is able to lay claim to at least one Russell Group university.[114] If the students graduating from these universities were to remain located around the country, it would promote a more equal spread of talent, and thus potential economic strength. However, this does not typically occur.

First of all, as one might expect, London retains its student base far better than other cities. One recent survey found that roughly seven in 10 final year degree students in London plan to remain in the capital once they have finished their studies. The English region with the next highest proportion of students intending to remain where they were being educated was the North West, but the total was fewer than three in ten believing they would.[115] Figures fall even further in other regions – only 12 per cent and 17 per cent of students in the East of England and the West Midlands, respectively.

London also acts as a magnet for talented people who had been studying elsewhere around the country. Another study found that the capital draws in 38 per cent of all new working graduates who left a Russell Group university with a first or upper second class degree. The phenomenon is even more pronounced for Oxbridge graduates, with 52 per cent of those with a first or upper second class degree moving to London.[116]

As a result, London has the largest share of graduates as a proportion of its population compared to any other region of the country – with some 56 per cent of Londoners educated at least to degree level.[117]

Surveying graduates about their reasons for moving to London and the South East reveals that they tend to move there because that is where the jobs they want are situated, and where the higher salaries can be found.[118] Again, this is a case of a self-fulfilling prophecy – because London and South East is already more prosperous and has more, better paid jobs, it attracts the top talent.

This is equally true for foreign talent. More international students enrol in London's universities than the combined totals for the whole of the North East, South West, Wales, East Midlands, East of England, and Northern Ireland.[119] This issue is exacerbated by the fact that many regional institutions have chosen to set up 'outposts' in the capital to attract students from around the world, with universities including Warwick, Loughborough and the West of Scotland being among those with London bases.[120]

The country does, of course, benefit from the cluster effect that results, with lots of bright and highly educated people flocking to work together. But without putting up roadblocks along various motorways bound for London, it is still possible to provide greater incentives for students to remain close to their almae matres upon graduation.

---

113   Times Higher Education, "World University Rankings 2019". Link.

114   Russell Group, "Our universities". Link.

115   Grant Thornton, "UK regions struggling to retain young talent". Link.

116   Paul Swinney and Marie Williams, "The Great British Brain Drain". Link.

117   ONS, "Graduates in the UK labour market: 2017". Link.

118   Ibid.

119   HESA, "Figure 6 – HE student enrolments by HE provider and domicile 2016/17". Link.

120   The Economist, "Seeking students and status, regional universities set up in London". Link.

Data suggests that a majority of students who get part-time jobs while at university do so to boost their employment prospects after they graduate.[121] While an educational purist may lament the ostensible marketisation of HE, students participating in economic activities while at university, like getting a job or undertaking an internship, might provide a means to level up the economy – particularly if they then stay in the area after graduating. It is important, then, that students are able to forge relationships with local employers prior to graduating, rather than attempting to do so in the short period of time after graduating and likely moving to another part of the country (particularly London).

We believe that the Office for Students should work with closely with universities, encouraging them to promote their students to local businesses, and local businesses to their students. Some universities, of course, do some of this already, but a more formal expectation should fall on universities – which are, ultimately, in receipt of billions of taxpayers' money each year[122] – to ensure that those students who wish to engage with local employers are helped to do so.

This measure should increase economic activity across the breadth of the country while students read for their degrees, but also serve to embed individuals into their local economies at the same time. This could help to stem the evident brain drain from places like Manchester, Newcastle, Belfast and Cardiff to London and the South East.

Other policies specifically targeted at helping graduates to work in deprived areas should also be explored by the

government. It is widely understood that, on average, graduates command higher salaries.[123] Given their greater earnings, it is intuitive that graduates have the potential to positively influence local economies. We recommend that both central and local governments consider fiscal measures to attract graduates into challenged areas, such as varying student loan repayments, or granting partial or full council tax exemptions – which could easily be done by amending the Council Tax (Discounts Disregards) Order 1992.[124] Where these measures take place would ideally be based on economic need – or they could work in tandem with the Opportunity Zones we recommend in this report.

Improving skills across the nation

It would be narrow-minded to think graduates alone can provide the solution to the long-term skills shortage in certain parts of the UK. Successive governments have waxed lyrical about the importance of vocational education, principally delivered by Further Education colleges. But it is widely recognised that this is an area that has been neglected compared to its more illustrious relation, HE.

Getting the provision of Further Education and lifelong learning right is critical to the future success, and regional spread, of the British economy. The challenges in this area are well known and numerous. Many employers say they cannot access the skills they need; many employees recognise they do not have the skills they require;[125] and it is obvious to many that the current system tends to be too supply-led rather than meeting employer demand.[126]

121 Natalie Gil, "One in seven students work full-time while they study". Link.

122 Paul Bolton, "Student loan statistics". Link.

123 Universities UK, "The economic impact of universities in 2014-15". Link.

124 The Council Tax (Discounts Disregards) Order 1992, No. 548. Link.

125 Chartered Institute of Personnel and Development, "From 'inadequate' to 'outstanding': making the UK's skills system world class". Link.

126 Sandy Leitch, "Leitch Review of Skills: Prosperity for all in the global economy – world class skills". Link.

These challenges are only likely to become more challenging especially amid the context of automation, which poses both opportunities and threats to the workforce.[127] The changing nature of economies around the world is likely to mean we are going to need more people working in cyber-technology, space, virtual reality, augmented reality and biotechnology to name but a few sectors – industries in which the UK clearly needs to train more people to meet future need.

So it is a matter of some concern, as the Augar Review recently argued, that successive Governments have not prioritised FE in the way they should. Budgets have been falling: total spending on adult skills dropped by approximately 45 per cent in real terms between 2009/10 and 2017/18, with capital spending far behind where it should be.[128]

Not only should the government therefore embark upon the capital investment programme into FE colleges which the Augar Review called for, but it should also reconsider how the Apprenticeship Levy – the means by which the Government shifted the emphasis for funding skills training and provision onto industry – operates.

Ensuring we have the employees with the right skills for the British economy means continuing to prioritise advanced manufacturing and other STEM fields, including investing in apprenticeships. But apprenticeships are not the only model by which training can be provided and, even it if were, the current system by which the Apprenticeship Levy operates is not as effective as it should be.

The overall amount of funds garnered through the Apprenticeship Levy began at £2.3 billion in 2017-18. It is expected to raise as much as £3.3 billion by 2023-24.[129] By September 2018, employers had accumulated a total pot of £2.7 billion that they could draw down to pay for apprenticeship training – but many employers say the way in which the money can be spent is too restrictive. The statistics bear this out: after 18 months of operation, those employers had used only £370 million, or 13.7 per cent, of the pot.[130]

The Recruitment and Employment Confederation estimates that 670 of its members paid over £110 million into the Levy last year, but are unable to use most of that money, with 47 per cent unable to use any of the funds. This is despite eight in ten employers highlighting the importance of training and upskilling opportunities in boosting staff productivity.[131]

The Government should therefore overhaul the Apprenticeship Levy so that there is flexibility in how it is used, particularly in the most disadvantaged areas. In particular, funds from the Apprenticeship Levy should be used as an employer desires, provided it is spent on skills and training, within Opportunity Zones or other areas which desperately need to see additional higher quality skills provision. This flexibility should pique the interest of employers and encourage them to invest in skills provision outside of London and the South East.

Adjustments also need to be made to ensure the Levy – and skills provision more generally – better supports the services-heavy nature of the UK economy.

---

127 Business, Energy and Industrial Strategy Select Committee, "Automation and the future of work". Link.

128 Department for Education, "Independent panel report to the Review of Post-18 Education and Funding". Link.

129 Office for Budget Responsibility, "March 2019 Economic and fiscal outlook – supplementary fiscal tables: receipts and other". Link.

130 Andy Powell, "Apprenticeships and skills policy in England". Link.

131 Recruitment and Employment Confederation, "Training for temps: Broadening the apprenticeship levy to benefit flexible workers". Link.

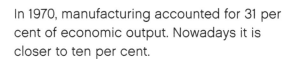

In 1970, manufacturing accounted for 31 per cent of economic output. Nowadays it is closer to ten per cent.

Currently, in most UK regions, workforce jobs are split roughly 80 per cent to 20 per cent in favour of the service sector – as illustrated in Chart 11, below. In London, fully 91 per cent of jobs are in services and the South East is second on 85 per cent.

Not only are more and more jobs being generated from within the service sector, but it is also where increased productivity and growth can be found. According to the ONS, output in the first quarter of 2016 from the service sector was 11.2 per cent higher than it was eight years previously, whereas production and construction were 7.4 per cent and 2.1 per cent lower respectively.[132]

Prima facie, then, there is a case for trying to increase service sector jobs outside London. These are clearly better paid, and more productive on the whole.

Yes, in part, this might be result of the agglomeration effect of living in London – and many of the other recommendations within this report will, it is to be hoped, help pave the way for similar (if weaker) agglomeration effects around the UK.[133]

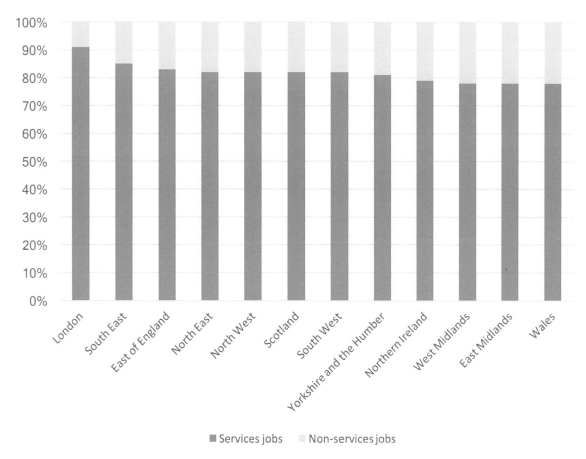

Chart 11. Workforce jobs, by region and industry (June 2019)

■ Services jobs ■ Non-services jobs

Source: ONS, "JOBS05: Workforce jobs by region and industry". Link.

---

132 ONS, "Five facts about... The UK service sector". Link.
133 Gilles Duranton and William R. Kerr, "The Logic of Agglomeration". Link.

But it is also because London appears to have more people with the requisite skills.

Once again, the rest of the country needs to play catch up, lest it runs the risk of being further left behind by the capital – and a more flexible use of the Levy outside of London and the South East should help in that regard.

There are plenty of examples of how spending the Levy is failing to work in some service industries. For example, temporary workers tend to get locked out of the scheme because their contracts do not meet the 12-month minimum requirement. The Government should therefore consider allowing the Apprenticeship Levy to be used entirely flexibly on skills and training provision by those companies operating in services outside of London and the South

East. That should include considering how those funds can be used to support reskilling and upskilling as part of a wider push on lifelong learning, in FE and HE institutions alike.

Providing this sort of flexibility, especially in those areas most in need of economic development, could help redress the balance and improve both skills and the service economy in the parts of the country which feel the need for them most keenly.

Conclusion

The United Kingdom has been economically unbalanced for too long, with the scales seemingly tipping ever further towards London and the South East in recent decades.

There are many reasons this imbalance began to manifest itself, but the capital's dominance appears to have become something of a self-fulfilling prophecy. Because London and its environs offer the best jobs, salaries and prospects, they Hoover up talent, attract the lion's share of public and private investment and maintain their grip on economic opportunity.

Throughout this report we have maintained that economic imbalance is not inherently bad. Indeed, in the relatively liberal and open economy which Britain is so fortunate to have, some degree of difference in outcome is inevitable. Yet, where imbalance becomes too great, the results can be pernicious for the rest of the country. Indeed, what might feel like a virtuous circle for London and the South East could lead to the precise opposite effect in other parts of the country: a seemingly inexorable decline in which a lack of opportunity leads to young people leaving, employers turning a blind eye and infrastructure investments being judged to not offer 'value for money' based on existing economic activity.

So, in particular where economic imbalance has come about a consequence of government policy, there is just cause to act.

For too long the Government has talked a good game on economic rebalancing, but to little avail. Fine words do butter no parsnips, as the phrase goes. But the new Prime Minister and Chancellor appear to be wholly serious in their determination to 'level up' the British economy. They have made positive noises about devolution, infrastructure and other means by which economically depressed areas might rise again. They have not yet, however, matched their ambitions with a fully fleshed-out strategy and a set of interventions which could really make a difference. This report aims to do precisely that.

This report contains a series of recommendations which we believe are credible and which would effectively redress disparities in the UK's economy. It is a plan to reset historic imbalances, allowing everybody to fulfil their potential, regardless of the corner of the country in which they happen to reside.

We are confident these ideas are also politically salient – both within Westminster and among the wider public. Levelling up the economy along the lines we set out, can, we believe, unleash dormant prosperity in regions where before it has been lacking, while maintaining the coveted strength of the nation's existing economic powerhouses – ensuring that a rising tide truly can lift all boats.

Bibliography

Adam Smith, *An Inquiry into the Nature and Causes of the Wealth of Nations*, 1776.

Aileen Murphie, *Learning lessons from LEPs*, 2019.

Alex Hill, Liz Mellon, Jules Goddard and Ben Laker, *How to Turn Around a Failing School*, 2016.

Andy Powell, *Apprenticeships and skills policy in England*, 2019.

B.R. Mitchell, *The Coming of the Railway and United Kingdom Economic Growth*, 1964.

BBC, *'Startling turnaround' transforms London state schools*, 2012.

BBC, *Edinburgh 'tourist tax' backed by council*, 2019.

Ben Gardiner, *The UK – an imbalanced economy*, 2019.

Business, Energy and Industrial Strategy Select Committee, *Automation and the future of work*, 2019.

Cabinet Office and Prime Minister's Office, 10 Downing Street, *Queen's Speech 2019*, 2019.

Centre for Cities, *Devolution and exiting the EU: Written evidence to the Public Administration and Constitutional Affairs Committee*, 2018.

Chartered Institute of Personnel and Development, *From 'inadequate' to 'outstanding': making the UK's skills system world class*, 2017.

Chris Cook, *London schools rise to the challenge*, 2012.

Civil Engineers Contractors Association, *Securing our economy: The case for infrastructure*, 2013.

Colin Copus and Steve Leach, *Let's talk about tax*, 2019.

Conrad Quilty-Harper, *Mapped: how the country's population changes during a work day*, 2013.

Core Cities UK, *A call for Greater Fiscal Autonomy of our Cities*, 2016.

Department for Business, Innovation and Skills and HM Treasury, *Government's response to the Heseltine review into economic growth*, 2013.

Department for Education, *£30,000 starting salaries proposed for teachers*, 2019.

Department for Education, *Independent panel report to the Review of Post-18 Education and Funding*, 2019.

Department for Education, *National curriculum assessments at key stage 2 in England, 2018 (provisional)*, 2018.

Department for Education, *Revised GCSE and equivalent results in England, 2016 to 2017*, 2018.

Department for International Trade, *Britain's Trading Future*, 2018.

Department for International Trade, *Inward Investment Results 2015/16*, 2016.

Department for International Trade, *Inward Investment Results 2016-17*, 2017.

Department for International Trade, *Inward Investment Results 2017-18*, 2018.

Department for International Trade, *Inward Investment Results 2018-19*, 2019.

Department for International Trade, *Trade and Investment Core Statistics Book*, 2019.

Department for Transport, *Government sets out next steps for Heathrow expansion*, 2018.

Department for Work and Pensions, *Development of a new measure of poverty: statistical notice*, 2019.

Eamonn Ives, *Tipping the Balance: How trade and investment can rebalance the UK economy*, 2019.

Enrico Moretti, *The New Geography of Jobs*, 2013.

Eric Ohrn, *The Effect of Tax Incentives on U.S. Manufacturing: Evidence from State Accelerated Depreciation Policies*, 2017.

European Investment Bank, *Financed projects*, 2019.

Eurostat, *GDP at regional level*, 2019.

Ferdinand Mount, *Prime Movers*, 2018.

Fiona Morrill, *Devolving other national taxes to London*, 2017.

Francisco Alcalá and Antonio Ciccone, *Trade and Productivity*, 2004.

Friedrich Hayek, *The Use of Knowledge in Society*, 1945.

Gareth Campbell, Meeghan Rogers and John Turner, *The Rise and Decline of the UK's Provincial Stock Markets, 1869-1929*, 2016.

Gerard Turnbull, *Canals, Coal and Regional Growth during the Industrial Revolution*, 1987.

Gilles Duranton and William R. Kerr, *The Logic of Agglomeration*, 2015.

Government Office for Science, *Governance of UK Transport Infrastructure*, 2019.

Grant Thornton, *UK regions struggling to retain young talent*, 2018.

Great Western Cities, *Britain's Western Powerhouse*, 2016.

Greater Manchester Combined Authority, *Greater Manchester City Deal*, 2012.

Gregory Clark and Neil Cummins, *Surnames and Social Mobility: England 1230-2012*, 2013.

Gregory Clark and Neil Cummins, *The Big Sort: Selective Migration and the Decline of Northern England, 1800-2017*, 2017.

H.B. Rodgers, *The Lancashire Cotton Industry in 1840*, 1960.

Hansjörg Blöchliger and José Maria Pinero Campos, *Tax Competition Between Sub-Central Governments*, 2011.

Hansjörg Blöchliger and Oguzhan Akgun, *Fiscal decentralisation and economic growth*, 2018.

Helen Johnson, *Metrolink has been voted one of the world's best tram systems – but here's what you think about it*, 2019.

HESA, *Figure 6 – HE student enrolments by HE provider and domicile 2016/17*, 2018.

HM Government, *Industrial Strategy: Building a Britain fit for the future*, 2017.

HM Revenue and Customs, *UK Regional Trade in Goods Statistics*, 2019.

HM Treasury and the Department for Business, Innovation and Skills, *The Plan for Growth*, 2011.

HM Treasury and the Department for International Trade, *Trade Secretary announces Freeports Advisory Panel will ensure UK is ready to trade post-Brexit*, 2019.

HM Treasury and the Infrastructure and Projects Authority, *Infrastructure Finance Review: consultation*, 2019.

HM Treasury, *Country and regional analysis: November 2017*, 2017.

HM Treasury, *Fixing the foundations: Creating a more prosperous nation*, 2015.

HM Treasury, the Department for Digital, Culture, Media and Sport, and the Department for Business, Energy and Industrial Strategy, *Chancellor announces support for post-Brexit future*, 2019.

House of Commons Library, *"A process, not an event": Devolution in Wales, 1998-2018*, 2018.

House of Commons Library, *Devolution to local government in England*, 2019.

Infrastructure and Projects Authority, *Analysis of the National Infrastructure and Construction Pipeline*, 2018.

Inland Revenue Service, *Opportunity Zones Frequently Asked Questions*, 2019.

Institute for Fiscal Studies, *Taking control: which taxes could be devolved to English local government?*, 2019.

Institute for Fiscal Studies, *Tax by design*, 2011.

Institute for Government, *How to value infrastructure: Improving cost benefit analysis*, 2017.

Institute for Government, *Tax and devolution*, 2018.

Institute for Government, *UK 'almost most centralised developed country', says Treasury chief*, 2015.

Institution of Civil Engineers, *State of the Nation 2018: Infrastructure Investment*, 2018.

Intellectual Property Office, *Facts and figures: Patent, trade mark, design and hearing administrative data 2016 and 2017 calendar years*, 2018.

International Monetary Fund, *Is it time for an infrastructure push? The macroeconomic effects of public investment*, 2014.

Jeffrey A. Frankel and David Romer, *Does Trade Cause Growth?*, 1999.

Jess Shankleman, *Boris Johnson Widens Push for Singapore-Style Free Ports in U.K.*, 2019.

Jo Blanden, Ellen Greaves, Paul Gregg, Lindsay Macmillan and Luke Sibieta, *Understanding the improved performance of disadvantaged pupils in London*, 2015.

John Bachtler, *Regional disparities in the United Kingdom*, 2004.

John Johnston, *Boris Johnson vows to create thousands more school places in bid to 'drive up standards'*, 2019.

Jonathan Dupont, *Powering the Midlands Engine: How to build a local Industrial Strategy*, 2018.

Lahari Ramuni, *Myth #11: Bringing back manufacturing will make Britain great again*, 2018.

London First, *The role of private capital in securing London's future infrastructure*, 2019.

Marc Kidson and Emma Norris, *Implementing the London Challenge*, 2014.

Matt Wheartly, *How do cities trade with the world? An analysis of the export profile of Britain's cities*, 2019.

Matthew Daley, *Options for a tourism levy for London*, 2017.

Matthew Ward, *Enterprise Zones*, 2016.

Mayor of London and Transport for London, *Strategic Cycling Analysis: Identifying future cycling demand in London*, 2017.

Merryn Hutchins, *Why is attainment higher in London than elsewhere?*, 2013.

Merryn Somerset Webb, *A Scottish stock exchange: an idea whose time has come?*, 2019.

Michael Heseltine, *No stone unturned: in pursuit of growth*, 2012.

Michael Kitson and Jonathan Michie, *The Deindustrial Revolution: The Rise and Fall of UK Manufacturing, 1870-2010*, 2014.

Ministry of Housing Communities and Local Government, *The New Enterprise Zones*, 2015.

Ministry of Housing, Communities and Local Government, *TheCityUK National Conference 2018*, 2018.

Minoo Farhadi, *Transport infrastructure and long-run economic growth in OECD countries*, 2015.

Muhammad Ali, Abiodun Egbetokun and Mazoor Hussain Memom, *Human Capital, Social Capabilities and Economic Growth*, 2018.

Natalie Gil, *One in seven students work full-time while they study*, 2014.

National Assembly for Wales, *The History of Welsh Devolution*, 2019.

National Audit Office, *Managing the expansion of the Academies Programme*, 2013.

National Audit Office, *The Academies Programme*, 2010.

National Foundation for Educational Research, *Key insights for PISA 2015 for the UK nations*, 2016.

National Infrastructure Commission, *National Infrastructure Assessment*, 2018.

Neil O'Brien, *Firing on all cylinders: Building a strong economy from the bottom up*, 2019.

Nicholas Apergis, Oguzhan Dincer and James Payne, *Economic freedom and income inequality revisited: Evidence from a panel error correction model*, 2013.

Nicholas Crafts, *Regional GDP in Britain, 1871-1911: Some estimates*, 2004.

Nicholas Crafts, *Transport infrastructure and investment: implications for growth and productivity*, 2009.

Nick King, *Think Small: A blueprint for support UK small businesses*, 2019.

Nicole Gicheva, Nigel Keohane and Scott Corfe, *Making apprenticeships work*, 2019.

Northern Ireland Office, *The Belfast Agreement*, 1998.

OECD, *Fostering Investment in Infrastructure: Lessons learned from OECD Investment Policy Reviews*, 2015.

OECD, *Programme for International Student Assessment (PISA) results from PISA 2015: United Kingdom*, 2016.

OECD, *Revenue Statistics 2018: Tax revenue trends in the OECD*, 2018.

OECD, *Trade in goods and services*, 2019.

Office for Budget Responsibility, *March 2019 Economic and fiscal outlook – supplementary fiscal tables: receipts and other*, 2019.

Office for the Secretary of State for Wales, *Welsh Secretary – "Now is the time to create our own Western Powerhouse"*, 2018.

ONS, *Annual Survey of Hours and Earnings time series of selected estimates*, 2018.

ONS, *Business enterprise research and development*, UK: 2017, 2018.

ONS, *Estimates of the population for the UK, England and Wales, Scotland and Northern Ireland: Mid-2017*, 2018.

ONS, *Five facts about... the UK services sector*, 2016.

ONS, *Graduates in the UK labour market: 2017*, 2017.

ONS, *JOBS05: Workforce jobs by region and industry*, 2019.

ONS, *Regional gross disposable household income by local authority*, 2018.

ONS, *Regional gross value added (income approach)*, 2018.

ONS, *Regionalised estimates of UK services exports*, 2018.

Paul Bolton, *Student loan statistics*, 2019.

Paul Swinney and Marie Williams, *The Great British Brain Drain*, 2016.

Philip Brien, *Public spending by country and region*, 2018.

Philip Hammond, *Remit letter for National Infrastructure Commission (NIC)*, 2019.

Philip McCann, *The UK Regional-National Economic Problem: Geography, Globalisation and Governance*, 2016.

Pierre Bessard, *Tax Competition: The Swiss Case*, 2008.

Prime Minister's Office, 10 Downing Street, *Boris Johnson's first speech as Prime Minister: 24 July 2019*, 2019.

Priti Patel, *Changing Gear: A Growth Budget to Drive the UK Economy*, 2019.

Recruitment and Employment Confederation, *Training for temps: Broadening the apprenticeship levy to benefit flexible workers*, 2019.

Revolution, *Rise of the Rest Seed Fund*, 2019.

Rishi Sunak, *The Free Ports Opportunity: How Brexit could boost trade, manufacturing and the North*, 2016.

Ron Martin, Andy Pike, Pete Tyler and Ben Gardiner, *Spatially rebalancing the UK economy: the need for a new policy model*, 2015.

Ron Martin, *The Political Economy of Britain's North-South Divide*, 1988.

Royal Academy of Engineering, *Crossrail: Delivering Europe's largest infrastructure project*, 2013.

Russell Group, *Our universities*, 2019.

Sam Bowman, *Full expensing: The best idea you've never heard of*, 2017.

Sandy Leitch, *Prosperity for all in the global economy – world class skills*, 2006.

Scott Eastman and Nicole Kaeding, *Opportunity Zones: What We Know and What We Don't*, 2019.

Scott Eastman, *Measuring Opportunity Zone Success*, 2019.

Suella Braverman, *Fight for Free Schools*, 2019.

Tax Policy Center, *Briefing Book: A citizen's guide to the fascinating (though often complex) elements of the federal Tax System*, 2018.

Tax Policy Center, *How did the Tax Cuts and Jobs Act change business taxes?*, 2018.

The Conservative and Unionist Party, *Forward, Together: Our Plan for a Stronger Britain and a Prosperous Future*, 2017.

The Economist, *How Norman rule reshaped England*, 2016.

The Economist, *Seeking students and status, regional universities setting up in London*, 2019.

The King's Fund, *The London Challenge*, 2015.

The Scottish Parliament, *Devolved powers*, 2018.

The Scottish Parliament, *Past and Present*, 2019.

The Scottish Parliament, *What are the powers of the Scottish Parliament*, 2019.

Tim Leunig and James Swaffield, *Cities Unlimited: Making urban regeneration work*, 2007.

Times Higher Education, *World University Rankings 2019*, 2019.

Tony McAleavy and Alex Elwick, *School improvement in London: a global perspective*, 2016.

Transport for Greater Manchester, *Greater Manchester Transport Strategy 2040: Draft Delivery Plan (2020-2025)*, 2019.

Universities UK, *The economic impact of universities in 2014-15*, 2017.

UK2070 Commission, *Fairer and stronger: Rebalancing the UK economy*, 2019.

World Bank, *Doing Business 2019*, 2019.

World Bank, *GDP (current US$)*, 2019.

World Economic Forum, *The Global Competitiveness Report 2018*, 2018.

WPI Economics, *Brain gain: the role of homes and place making in attracting graduates to the North of England*, 2016.